CANCER
22 JUNE – 23 JULY

First published in Great Britain 2011
by Mills & Boon, an imprint of Harlequin (UK) Limited,
Eton House, 18-24 Paradise Road, Richmond, Surrey TW9 1SR

Copyright © Dadhichi Toth 2011

ISBN: 978 0 263 89654 1

Design by Jo Yuen Graphic Design
Typeset by KDW DESIGNS

Harlequin (UK) policy is to use papers that are natural, renewable and recyclable products and made from wood grown in sustainable forests. The logging and manufacturing processes conform to the legal environmental regulations of the country of origin.

Printed and bound in Spain
by Blackprint CPI, Barcelona

Dedicated to

The Light of Intuition

Sri V. Krishnaswamy—mentor and friend

With thanks to

Joram and Isaac

Special thanks to

Nyle Cruz for

initial creative layouts and ongoing support

⦿ ABOUT DADHICHI ⦿

Dadhichi is one of Australia's foremost astrologers and is frequently seen on television and in other media. He has the unique ability to draw from complex astrological theory to provide clear, easily understandable advice and insights for people who want to know what their futures may hold.

In the 26 years that Dadhichi has been practising astrology, face reading and other esoteric studies, he has conducted over 10,000 consultations. His clients include celebrities, political and diplomatic figures, and media and corporate identities from all over the world.

Dadhichi's unique blend of astrology and face reading helps people fulfil their true potential. His extensive experience practising Western astrology is complemented by his research into the theory and practice of Eastern forms of astrology.

Dadhichi has been a guest on many Australian television shows, and several of his political and worldwide forecasts have proved uncannily accurate. He appears regularly on Australian television networks and is a columnist for online and offline Australian publications.

His websites—www.dadhichi.com and www.facereader. com—attract hundreds of thousands of visitors each month, and offer a wide variety of features, helpful information and services.

MESSAGE FROM
◎ DADHICHI ◎

Hello once again and welcome to your 2012 horoscope book!

Can you believe it's already 2012? Time flies by so quickly and now here we are in this fateful year, a time for which several religions of the world—including the Mayans from 3100BC—have predicted some extraordinary events that are supposedly going to affect us all!

Some people are worried there will be a physical cataclysm that will kill millions and millions. Some are of the opinion it is the end of the economic and social models we have lived by for thousands of years. Others seem to believe the Planet Nibiru will whiz by planet Earth and beam up the 144,000 Chosen Ones.

Whatever the opinion, it is an undeniable fact that we are experiencing some remarkable worldwide changes due to global warming (even though that remains a point of contention) and other societal shifts. Scientific knowledge continues to outrun our ability to keep up with it, and time appears to be moving faster and faster.

But my own research has categorically led me to repeat: 'Relax, everyone; it is *not* the end of the world!' There will most certainly be a backlash at some point by Mother Earth at the gross unconsciousness of many of us. There will be ravaging storms, earthquakes and other meteorological phenomena that will shake the Earth, hopefully waking up those of us still in a deep sleep, dreaming, or possibly even sleepwalking. It is time to open our eyes and take responsibility.

If there are any significant global changes I foresee, they are the emergence of wider self-government and the greater Aquarian qualities of the coming New Age. This period is the cusp or changeover between the Age of Pisces, the Fish, and the Age of Aquarius, the Dawn of Higher Mankind.

Astrology, and these small books I write about it, are for the sole purpose of shedding light on our higher selves, alerting us to the need to evolve, step up to the plate, and assume responsibility for our thoughts, words and deeds, individually and collectively. The processes of karma are ripe now as we see the Earth's changes shouting to us about our past mistakes as a civilisation.

I hope you gain some deeper insight into yourself through these writings. For the 2012 series I have extended the topics and focused more on relationships. It is only through having a clear perception of our responsibility towards others that we can live the principles of astrology and karma to reach our own self-actualisation, both as individuals and as a race.

I hope you see the light of truth within yourself and that these words will act as a pointer in your ongoing search.

All the best for 2012.

Your Astrologer,

www.dadhichi.com
dadhichitoth@gmail.com
Tel: +61 (0) 413 124 809

◎ CONTENTS ◎

⊚ CONTENTS ⊚

☺ CONTENTS ☺
CONTINUED

2012: Monthly and Daily Predictions

2012: Astronumerology

CANCER
PROFILE

YOU'RE ONLY GIVEN A LITTLE SPARK
OF MADNESS. YOU MUSTN'T LOSE IT.

Robin Williams

CANCER
◎ SNAPSHOT ◎

Key Life Phrase		I Nurture
Zodiac Totem		The Crab
Zodiac Symbol		♋
Zodiac Facts		Fourth sign of the zodiac; cardinal, fruitful, feminine and moist
Zodiac Element		Water
Key Characteristics		Loving, susceptible, sympathetic, sensual, faithful, instinctive, charitable, over-reactive and moody
Compatible Star Signs		Taurus, Virgo, Scorpio and Pisces

Mismatched Signs		Sagittarius, Capricorn, Aquarius and Libra
Ruling Planet		Moon
Love Planets		Mars and Pluto
Finance Planet		Sun
Speculation Planet		Mars
Career Planets		Neptune, Jupiter and Mars
Spiritual and Karmic Planets		Mars, Pluto, Jupiter and Neptune
Friendship Planet		Venus
Destiny Planet		Mars

Famous Cancers ★★	50 Cent, Jerry Hall, Vin Diesel, Tom Hanks, Josh Hartnett, Josh Holloway, Tobey Maguire, John Cusack, Robin Williams, Ringo Starr, Carlos Santana, Lindsay Lohan, Courtney Love, Liv Tyler, Kristen Bell, Sophia Bush, Ashley Tisdale, Selma Blair, Missy Elliott, Meryl Streep, Gisele Bündchen and Deborah Harry
Lucky Numbers and Significant Years	2, 3, 9, 11, 12, 18, 20, 21, 27, 29, 30, 36, 38, 45, 47, 48, 54, 56, 57, 74, 75, 81, 83 and 84
Lucky Gems	Moonstone, pearl, yellow topaz, red coral, garnet and white jade
Lucky Fragrances	Geranium, sandalwood, white rose, ylang ylang and bergamot
Affirmation/ Mantra	I am loveable as well as loving
Lucky Days	Monday, Tuesday and Thursday

CANCER
◎ OVERVIEW ◎

I don't think I've ever met a Cancer-born individual who didn't come across as trustful, reliable and genuine in the way they dealt with me. Mind you, if you're born under the sign of Cancer, I would say you're not an easy person to read—not initially, anyway. The main reason for this is probably linked to your zodiac totem, the Crab. I've made reference to this in my previous books, how the hard exterior of this crustacean often shrouds the softer and more sensual side of the Cancerian personality.

Being hard on the outside means you're able to test the waters with others before revealing the true depth of your emotions. And emotion is one of the key words for your star sign, there's no doubt about that. The Cancerian is a deep ocean of feeling, sensitivity and imagination. All of the water signs are. But you, Cancer, exhibit the additional astrological trait of mobility. This means the element of water is constantly moving and shifting in you, indicating the rulership of the Moon over your star sign.

The Moon regulates the tides, taking them out and bringing them in, day in and day out. Much like the inward and outward movement of the ocean, your feelings, tend to shift, bringing with them an element of moodiness and complication in your emotional life. You may not be easy to understand, and often people find it difficult to grasp why you exhibit the moods that you do.

MOODY CANCER!

*Moodiness doesn't necessarily entail a lack of
connectedness with others. Quite the contrary. You,
Cancer, are one of the most attached and reciprocal
star signs, giving back love and attention to those who
prove themselves worthy.*

Because Cancer rules the home, and is in particular the archetype of the mother, both men and women born under this water sign seem to excel at family life and raising children. You relish expressing your deep emotions and love by caring for and helping others. You are very charitable, and you possess an instinct for being able to pick just when someone needs your help, even if unasked for. Once again, this is the expression of the deep and intuitive water trait, which gives its natives their keen sensitivity and empathy for others.

Cancer's Kindness

You never forget a kindness or an offence. You retain things very much like a sponge retains water. Your memory is excellent, but this may also have its downside, in that you're not able to let go of things easily.

Another aspect of the Moon that doesn't always work well for you is its maternal nature. You sometimes veer too close to the mothering/smothering lane, which can put people off.

Back on the positives, you love to mix with all sorts of people. Social activities are an essential ingredient in your development. You are a great success socially because you convey your wisdom to others so well—Cancerians have very expressive faces.

You love to collect and keep mementoes, such as scrapbooks and other bits and pieces, which bring back memories of good times and people you care about. You have a great memory, not just for facts, but also for any good turn or kindness you've received.

You can always talk about any subject with anyone. Your retentive memory is a help here, as is your impartial, even-handed approach to people in general. Dealing with people comes naturally to you. Add this to your shrewdness and intuition, and you are likely to be a good businessperson. You can also use these skills in managing your day-to-day life.

You mustn't let phobias and fears, whether real or imaginary, undermine your great abilities and wonderful humanness. These self-doubts—or feelings of incompleteness and inadequacy—could well undo a lot of the great opportunities that you are destined to experience. Continue to trust your intuition, show your love, surmount these negative emotional traits, and you'll achieve wonderful things in your life.

◎ CANCER CUSPS ◎

ARE YOU A CUSP BABY?

Being born on the changeover of two star signs means you have the qualities of both. Sometimes you don't know whether you're Arthur or Martha, as they say! Some of my clients can't quite figure out if they are indeed their own star sign, or the one before, or after. This is to be expected because being born on the borderline means you take on aspects of both. The following outlines give an overview of the subtle effects of these cusp dates and how they affect your personality quite significantly.

Cancer–Gemini Cusp

I may have come across with an accusing tone when I talked previously about just how much feeling and emotion you possess. But if you're born on the cusp of Gemini, which is when your birth falls between the 22nd and the 29th or 30th of June, you will exhibit many of the intellectual traits of Gemini that can balance the over-emotionalism found in the typical Cancer.

The curiosity and mental brilliance of Gemini can counteract some of the emotional traits you possess, but at the same time, you may find it hard to make decisions. Your mind might clash with your heart, and this could cause you to procrastinate, especially when it comes to matters of love.

A CURIOUS CANCER?

*With all of this blending of intellectual and emotional
energies, it's no wonder you have this deep desire to
understand, to get to the bottom of why things are the
way they are. Understanding, spiritual insight and a
curiosity for human affairs will be at the heart of your
personality.*

You're a clever communicator and possess a
wonderful skill in being able to mediate for others.
Yours is the shoulder people cry on, not just because
you compassionately want to help them, but because
somehow you can clearly see a solution to the problem
at hand.

Cancer–Leo Cusp

Being born between the 16th or 17th and the 23rd of July
gives you a mixture of Cancer and Leo traits. With the
added zest of the fire sign of Leo, this makes you both
nurturing and homely, and a showman/showwoman,
of sorts. If you love to entertain, you will do so in the
comfort of your own home, which, I must add, would
indicate your houseproud nature.

The fire of Leo will heat up your nature considerably and
you must be careful not to let this spill over into your
emotional life. You could become extreme, demanding
and prone to dramatic outbursts if you don't get your
own way. Use the cool waters of your Cancerian Sun

sign to extinguish the overzealous fire of Leo.

Both Cancer and Leo are considered loyal and devoted star signs, and with the blending of these two, we see in you one of the most faithful people to know. In relationships—or friendships of any sort—people will see this part of your personality as one of your most endearing traits.

You are straightforward, non-deceptive and frank in all your dealings. If, however, someone does the wrong thing by you, you are likely to be unforgiving for a very long time. Such is the fixedness of Leo and the emotional intensity of Cancer when they mix.

Being born at the junction of these two star signs makes you particularly affectionate, warm and loving. You are ardently giving in your love, but expect the same sort of appreciation in return. If that love is reciprocated, the lucky giver will realise just what a great friend and confidant you are.

CANCER
⊚ CELEBRITIES ⊚

FAMOUS MALE:
VIN DIESEL

If I keep harping back to the tough exterior of the Cancerian crustacean totem, you'll understand why as we consider the male celebrity Vin Diesel, and discover just how misleading the outer personality of a Cancerian can be.

Like Burt Reynolds in the seventies, Clint Eastwood in the eighties, and Harrison Ford and Mel Gibson in the nineties, the hard, masculine, tough-as-nails persona of the present moment is Vin Diesel. But, of course, this is all Hollywood glam, and Vin Diesel, as a Cancer, would exhibit the caring and loving characteristics of those born under the nurturing sign of the Crab.

Here (as with Lindsay Lohan, below) we learn that Vin Diesel, born Mark Vincent on the 18th of July, 1967, never knew his biological father. This would have affected him deeply. It's ironic that Cancerian individuals, who thrive on family support networks, can reach such high-profile levels without this initial foundation in life. Vin Diesel has a twin brother and two younger siblings, and this whole family connectedness would have been an important cornerstone of his development.

I would say that with Vin Diesel—as with many other Cancerians—you should never judge a book by its cover.

VIN DIESEL'S MOTHER WAS AN ASTROLOGER!

Interestingly, his mother, Dolora, was an astrologer. She also achieved a Master's degree in psychology. Vin was lucky to have a woman like this as a mother. She would have brought his attention to his varied cultural roots, making him feel as if he did have an identity and wasn't completely devoid of a solid family foundation.

Due to Uranus's placement in his career zone in 2012, Vin will have some unexpected opportunities in his work. He may choose a role that is completely outside his usual character. Being an adaptable star sign, Cancer is able to adjust itself to the demands that may arise, and do a great job despite the challenges.

FAMOUS FEMALE:
LINDSAY LOHAN

There are not too many people around who haven't heard about the tumultuous life of Hollywood celebrity Lindsay D. Lohan. Lindsay, born on the 2nd of July, 1986, has been in the news for some time, in particular for her wild and rampant lifestyle involving the proverbial sex, drugs and rock 'n' roll.

There've been some rather harrowing times for Lindsay over the past few years, including several stays in prison and an inability to shake her wanton behaviour. The emotionalism of Cancer, when it gets out of hand, can be seen in some of the behaviour of Lindsay.

This also has something to do with the fact that many child stars, including Lindsay, find it hard to adjust themselves to society as they get older. Their relationships become dysfunctional, as do their family lives. In Lindsay's case, she was only three when she became a child model and commercial actress. She starred in over 60 television spots and 100 print advertisements for Toys 'R' Us and other leading manufacturers. In 1998, she appeared in the Disney remake of *The Parent Trap*.

Many of Lindsay's problems stem from her deep Cancerian emotionalism, probably from a misguided desire to receive the affection and attention that a typical Cancerian needs.

In becoming more and more famous, her visits to New York nightclubs and her wild party lifestyle brought her to the attention of the paparazzi. In 2007, she was arrested when she crashed her Mercedes Benz into a tree in a rich Hollywood suburb. Lindsay's need to balance her emotions typifies the complexities in the Cancerian personality.

The movement of Uranus through her career sector may not be a great thing in 2012, because it could unsettle her already floundering career. Lindsay seriously needs to take stock of where she is and what she wants to achieve at this stage of her life.

CANCER

AT LARGE

I AM NOT BOTHERED BY THE
FACT THAT I AM UNKNOWN. I AM
BOTHERED WHEN I DO NOT KNOW
OTHERS.

Confucius

☽ CANCER MAN ☽

♂

CANCER MAN: SNAPSHOT

Sensitive

Caring

Intuitive

Family-oriented

Well read

The male born under Cancer is one of the most reliable and devoted individuals you'll meet, priding himself on his ability to care for others. Not always showing his feelings can make him appear a bit of an enigma to others, which can cause them to withdraw in the mistaken belief that the Cancer man is unapproachable, elitist or a downright snob. This is, of course, not true at all, and when you dig a little deeper, you'll find that he isn't stuffy or condescending, just a little shy, and unable to express immediately the depth of feeling that is part of his temperament.

There's an element of sympathy and charity associated with you, if you happen to be a male Cancerian reading this. You know full well that charity begins at home, so you therefore make every effort possible to prove you're a good husband, father and provider for your family. You never ever take your responsibilities lightly, and those who know you understand that even if you don't earn a great deal, you consider that the greatest wealth is love, affection, support and devotion for the ones you love.

The Cancerian men that I've met most definitely have a soft heart, but, funnily enough, their heads can be a little bit hard, especially when challenged. If they lose an argument, or don't get their own way, they are (would you believe) sulkers, of sorts, and they can brood for days on end. Don't knock a Cancer man's nose out of joint or you'll suffer the repercussions for some time. They have a tendency to hold on to a grudge.

Although Cancers enjoy home life and nurturing the family, I must remind you that this is what's known as a moveable sign under the scheme of the astrological zodiac, and, in short, this reflects the Cancer male's need to understand the world, to travel, and to connect with others. Most of the Cancer men whom I've encountered have an extraordinary depth of knowledge, even if they don't happen to be formally educated.

In a nutshell, Cancer, you're loving, caring and able to support others, especially in their times of need.

There are, however, some personality flaws that you must guard against. Depending on your background, upbringing and, of course, the intensity of your Cancerian personality, you may have developed the tendency to be too needy. This can make others feel as if you cramp their style, so you must be careful to give them space, even if you feel a little insecure at times. You have to be careful not to develop feelings of envy or jealousy, especially with family members, as this can complicate your home life and push others away rather than draw them closer to you.

In respect of these issues, it's important to take the time to address them, which will only happen through a concerted effort at becoming more self-aware and observing others' reactions to you in day-to-day, real-life circumstances. If you take the time and make the effort to change this one aspect of neediness in your character, you'll find you'll be so much happier in your life.

GOOD OLD-FASHIONED CANCER

You may be a little old-fashioned in your approach to life, but you're as honest as the day is long. You are also temperamental from time to time, but people know exactly where they stand with you. These are two huge pluses.

Even if you have not had much formal education, you are very knowledgeable and will learn much on your path through life. You always have an interesting point of view on whatever topic is under discussion, and you are impartial, treating king and beggar alike.

You will attract women who are looking for a man who is family-oriented. You make a great husband, father and homemaker because you enjoy whipping up a meal and love spending time with children. All in all, you get a tick in every 'family life' box anyone can think of.

You are very determined about your ambitions, but you may have a number of big professional hurdles in your life.

One part of your key life lesson will be patience: if you wait, fortune will smile upon you. The other part will be about excessive emotionalism: learn to stay calm.

◎ CANCER WOMAN ◎

CANCER WOMAN: SNAPSHOT

Loving

Compassionate

Organised

Absorbs feelings

Family comes first

It's very hard to say no to any woman born under Cancer, especially when she shoves a piece of warm, home-baked apple pie and a cup of coffee in front of you when you least expect it. Such is the hospitality and mothering qualities of a woman born under this soft and giving sign.

You see, this tendency to give, nurture and mother is inherent in the star sign of Cancer. Astrology is replete with examples of how the Moon, ruler of this particular star sign, is endowed with the archetypal sovereignty over femininity, motherhood, love and family life. This is the reason, and the motivation, behind your desire to express the loving characteristic of your nature to everyone, not just family and friends. Your water sign is very much linked to the other water sign of Pisces, which is the most self-sacrificing of the star signs. You too possess this quality, and people will often note your selfless and humble service to strangers and those in need.

As a woman born under Cancer, the Moon will also reveal some of its changeable qualities in your personality, and you may not like this. In the ancient Sanskrit language, from which many of the Indo-European languages emerged, the word *manas* (or mind) is ruled by Chandra, the Moon. The intimate link between the quick-moving lunar cycle and the human mental and emotional state has been known for thousands of years in the ancient Vedic astrological tradition. Being born under the sign of the Moon will highlight the fact that your emotions and your mental traits are as quick-moving and changeable as the Earth's nearest neighbour.

Sometimes you are completely overwhelmed by your feelings and may not know how to deal with it. This is probably one reason why you opt for generosity, charity and compassion to others. In this way, you find a safe and acceptable outlet for a deluge of emotion. And, of course, this is a positive way in which you can express and successfully channel this kaleidoscope of feeling.

As a woman under Cancer, you also have an incredible imagination. Another way for you to let off steam, if I can put it that way, is to engage yourself in art, crafts and, of course, any home pastimes such as cooking, gardening and the like. This would be an excellent match for your Cancerian personality. Because cooking and handicrafts involve a high degree of care and love for others, you'll take to these activities like a duck to water.

You are a very receptive person. However, this is a double-edged sword, because you are intuitively able to feel the pulse of others and the prevailing trends, but may not quite know how to offload these moods once you take them on board. This is why for you, Cancer, your careful selection of friends and associates is all the more important.

By surrounding yourself with people who are negative in their attitudes, you will find your moods taking on the same colour. Selecting your friends wisely will have a remarkable, positive effect on you, especially if you choose only those people who have a good philosophy and attitude in life.

CANCER AND MOTHERHOOD

The Moon rules motherhood, family and nurturing.
You are strongly drawn to having a family, and you
flow into the role of mother easily. This means that
fleeting affairs are not for you. You are a traditionalist
at heart, someone for whom marriage is a sacrosanct
commitment.

You have powerful intuition—make sure you use it when you meet potential partners. You are likely to skip right over the negative side of people because you believe that there is something good in all of us. Well, yes and no. Trust your hunches and you'll avoid many pitfalls in your love life.

Family is also important to you as a way of expressing yourself, and you often show your feelings in quite a physical way. For you, it's pure indulgence to lavish warmth on your family and friends. You will find rearing children deeply fulfilling, but you will have trouble letting them go. You do tend to be clingy.

Because you are so busy taking care of your family and friends, you sometimes forget to look after yourself. You can end up procrastinating when it comes to your own self-improvement. Give yourself a little more love.

⊚ CANCER CHILD ⊚

You have to be a master psychologist to deal with the child of Cancer. If you happen to have a child who's born under this sign, you must remember the complexity of emotion and mind that I've already discussed, along with the fact that the Crab possesses some pretty formidable nippers which can really hurt if they do decide to attack.

Your Cancer child is elusive, intuitive, loving and also, at times, deceptive—as shown by the sideways walk of the Crab. Your little crustacean will sometimes appear to act a little differently, but if you quiz them, they may never tell you the reason. Beneath their solemn and moody changes of mind, you'll often wonder what motivates them and why they are behaving the way they do. As I said, if you're a master psychologist and you have the time to work it out (and even then you may never understand it), you'll be a lucky parent. For the rest of you, your children will grow up, and that sort of behaviour may forever remain a mental teaser.

One thing you will notice about a Cancerian child, especially when they mix with their peers, is their incredibly open and sharing attitude. They are, on this point, exemplary. If, for example, a friend doesn't have a toy that your child does, your Cancerian kid will more than happily share it with them, even to their own detriment. They have an instinctive ability to open their hearts and look towards treating others with equality.

If their friends knew that to hurt a Cancerian is a pretty grave mistake, they would never do it. Your Cancerian child can be wounded deeply and, in some cases, be very unforgiving. This could account for one of the times when you can't explain their sullen behaviour.

If, for example, your child is insulted, demeaned or bullied at school, their quiet and timid ways may make it difficult for them to share the pain or anguish, and you'll be none the wiser. In these instances, you'll need to delve deep, and be unrelenting to get to the bottom of things, as the last thing you want is for your child to grow up shouldering that sort of burden. There's no doubt that this will impact heavily upon their relationships as they mature.

Bright Sparks

Because the Cancerian child is endowed with great intuition, a fine imagination, and a curious and creative streak, they generally enjoy learning and are good at retaining information. They may find it hard to grasp things at first, but repetition will result in greater retention. So never avoid or dismiss their need for a little extra tuition on the educational side of things.

One of the most important things is for your Cancerian child to have a sense of belonging, a soft place to fall. The impact of divorce and broken homes on children is obvious, but on a Cancerian child it is even more pronounced. Do your best to give them the nurturing, loving and stable home life that all children deserve and—in particular for Cancerian children—need.

⊙ CANCER LOVER ⊙

❝ YOU MUST LOOK INTO OTHER PEOPLE AS WELL AS AT THEM. (LORD CHESTERFIELD)❞

C♋

It's hard for any of us to deny that love, emotion and warmth of feeling make up the foundation for caring and enduring relationships. Cancer-born individuals are governed so strongly by this sense of feeling and emotion that they are natural lovers, through and through. You will relate completely to what I'm saying, Cancer, when I refer to the fact that, as an emotional star sign, you take the view that love is forever.

But there are some problems entertaining the idealistic level of love that you aspire to.

You don't function well when your emotions are disconnected from the physical act of love. I speak here particularly of sexuality. In this respect, sex without an outpouring of feeling is a dried and mechanical experience that in no way attracts you.

Penetrating your hard exterior is difficult for others, and those who are impatient may not take the time to work through that. Of course, you need to protect yourself and test those who suggest they want to give it a go with you in a romantic way. But you are not that easy, and want to test the waters of love significantly before giving your heart to someone unconditionally. That's the problem. You mustn't be shy in letting a prospective lover know that this is your way. At least if they understand where you're coming from, they may be happy to extend their patience, because what can be achieved once they do win your heart is very, very special.

As I said, it's an instinctive thing for you to love, and once you choose an individual, they are regarded as special, and are pampered, nourished and mothered in every way possible. In fact, the Cancer lover is in many ways the ideal lover. One of your requirements for love is that you find someone who not only satisfies your emotional and physical needs, but your practical and family needs as well. You want to know that your partner will step up to the plate, take the challenge, and share the load in making a nest and growing a family. You very much admire a partner who, like yourself, values the traditional concepts of family and the associated roles of parenthood.

It's very important that you pay close attention to what I'm about to say, Cancer, for this may have an important bearing upon your future happiness in relationships. And it is this: find a high degree of security within yourself before making that all-important commitment in love. If you're not able to feel empowered by your inner beauty and capacity in life, you may become insecure and demanding, expecting your partner to fulfil those things that you've never been able to achieve as an individual.

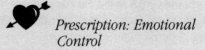

Prescription: Emotional Control

Once you gain control over the inner world of your emotions, you'll become the master of your destiny, and will be in the best position of all to enjoy romance and love.

Unfortunately, some Cancerians attract partners who are cold, aloof and distant. Think hard about the type of person with whom you want to spend your life. If they're not a major league hugger and kisser, you're going to get really frustrated. It's okay to trust your intuition in this area, but don't be afraid to use some good old brain power, too.

If you love someone but they don't love you back, you may go into a sullen, introverted, spiralling dive. You are quick to feel hurt, but sometimes you put your emotions in a sealed container and let them heat up to boiling point. Your lover will not know what is wrong, of course—they're not psychic! And this infuriates you even more. This is not a good cycle to get into.

The solution is to say how you feel before it gets on top of you. The lunar cycle will affect your mind and relationships, so learn to tune into your cycles. Once you recognise the signals, you'll be better able to handle what's happening, and share your feelings with your loved ones.

In so many cases I see this happening to you, Cancer, and it will become a key issue in your marriage or long-term relationships if you don't heed my advice. When your insecurities become overpowering, you'll find your moods dominating the landscape, causing you to sulk, retreat into yourself, and punish your partner with the silent treatment. You may end up using communication and silence as treat or punishment tools. Your partner may put up with this for some time, but in the end they will walk.

Taking a more spiritual view, remembering that your mind and emotions are your slaves and not your masters. This is the secret key to finding happiness in your relationships, and to not being pulled here, there and everywhere by changeable inner states.

⦿ CANCER FRIEND ⦿

The key word in any friendship has to be loyalty, and with Cancer, this comes naturally. Being the nurturers of the zodiac, they value friendship, but not necessarily in quantity so much as in quality.

You, Cancer, are able to make others feel great about themselves, and by taking interest in their lives, their circumstances and the highs and lows that come with life, you are appreciated as a great friend. Actually, you probably don't know it, but this one point—taking an interest in others, and not speaking so much about yourself—is a great secret to winning friends and influencing others. You've got it, and you may not have even realised it.

You are selfless in the way you approach friends, and when you regard someone this way, you will do anything for them. You realise that people want to be wanted and loved and to be made to feel good about themselves. And this you do in full measure with your friends.

You are irresistible because you really do want to help others and are genuinely interested in them. Your loving nature is a standout trait, and puts you in everyone's Top 10 as a friend and confidant. The way you share your feelings inspires others to do the same.

For some, this openness and warmth could mean being taken on a few rides. If you are an evolved Cancerian, though, it will mean quite the contrary. You are shrewd and perceptive when it comes to choosing friends and long-term partners, and use your intuition to understand people's motivations.

You have another great talent: an interest in general knowledge, which you put to use in very practical ways. You are keen to share this knowledge, and are never too proud to listen to another person's view (you may not take their advice, though!). Many Cancerians make their nurturing, never-say-no-to-anyone spirit the guiding direction for their lives.

What may surprise you at times (and this will probably happen over a longer period) is that as much as you give to others, you don't often find they reciprocate to the same extent. Have you ever wondered about this? Well, let me tell you one of the main reasons for this happening, Cancer. You have a tendency to hold much of your emotional inner life as private, even secret. When it comes to sharing how you feel—for whatever reason, maybe because you think you're imposing on others and don't want to burden them—people observe that you prefer them not to discuss this sacrosanct area of your life.

Eliciting generosity from your friends will require a greater degree of openness on your part. Perhaps not strangely, this involves trust. If you regard someone as a friend, and have done so for many, many years, they would like to feel as trusted as you do. It may take time for you to open up, but the more you do, the more you'll be able to deepen your friendship and ties of love with those who genuinely care as much for you as you do for them.

⊚ CANCER ENEMY ⊚

Those of you who have any sort of connection with Cancer may be well aware that the water sign of the Crab can, at times, be hypersensitive, and that anything you say can and will be used against you (although not necessarily in a court of law). I mention this because Cancerians do tend to concern themselves with trivia, and anything you say, which may seem quite harmless to you, can be blown out of proportion by them. This is where their irrational, merry-go-round type of thinking can build these harmless statements into something quite grandiose.

If, as a friend, you notice Cancer withdrawing, avoiding you and refusing to talk, then you can be pretty sure you've done something to offend them. You may already have become an enemy and don't yet know it. This passive-aggressive attitude can be quite disconcerting, especially if you approach them and they give you the cold shoulder. Once again, we see the sideways movement of the Crab in full swing under these circumstances.

The best advice is to let them get over it, if that's possible, and when the time's right, hopefully their caring nature will cause them to come back to you and give it a second go.

CANCER
AT HOME

THERE IS NO NEED FOR TEMPLES,
NO NEED FOR COMPLICATED
PHILOSOPHIES. MY BRAIN AND
MY HEART ARE MY TEMPLES; MY
PHILOSOPHY IS KINDNESS.

Dalai Lama

☺ HOME FRONT ☺

Having a warm, safe home environment is one of the key things on your agenda, Cancer. Your home is most definitely your castle, and although this applies to some of the other star signs of the zodiac as well, I can say unequivocally that, for you, this is the greatest priority. Your star sign stands out among all as one needing a safe haven from which to live life.

Feeling secure and comfortable means, however, that some of you born under this sign may tend to develop a stay-at-home mentality, sometimes preferring your own or your family's company to that of your social acquaintances, friends and workmates. Once again, I say that moderation and balance are the keys to a satisfactory lifestyle, and this case is no exception.

You need a safe haven, a place in which you can build up, collect and reminisce over your past. Many Cancerians like to display memorabilia, photographs and other artefacts that represent times in their past that trigger the warmest and most loving feelings.

Your decorating style could be considered conservative in many ways, but this is only because you believe furnishings and other possessions in the home should primarily be of a practical, if not emotional, nature. You like things to be useful, but at the same time you're not averse to simple, aesthetically pleasing shapes and forms. As an example, flowing lines in furniture will make you feel better generally. The warmer tones—creams and other comforting colours—are excellent for you.

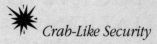

Crab-Like Security

The security aspect of your home once again represents that hard exterior that protects the inner, soft portion of the Crab. However, don't turn your home into a fortress, because this may have the effect of intimidating others when they come to visit.

Because the Moon is your ruling planet—and it is a water-related planet, at that—silver, milky and even watery colours, such as aqua and blue, will enhance your home decor. And wouldn't it be lovely if you had a skylight, which, on full Moon nights, would allow moonlight to stream into your home, giving you a sense of peace and spiritual awe?

We mustn't forget that the Moon rules the dark hours of night. As such, many of you born under the star sign of Cancer love to get creative at night. Thus, your home should reflect this tendency and accommodate your need to express and enjoy your life in the twilight hours.

HOME-STYLE LIVING A MUST

Cancers need a home that is inviting, warm and loving. Family-style living relaxes them and makes them feel fulfilled with their lot in life.

KARMA, LUCK AND
⊚ MEDITATION ⊚

Your past-life experiences colour and affect your current life circumstances. According to astrology, your soul is constantly evolving. The ninth sign from Cancer is Pisces, which is an important component of who you are in this life.

Because of this relationship, the watery and spiritual energies of the Neptune-ruled Pisces have much to do with your make-up. This is why Cancer is concerned with issues of spirituality and compassion. Part of the psychic nature of Pisces is deeply embedded in your character; it finds expression in your desire to make a meaningful life for yourself.

The water trinity—that is, Cancer, Scorpio and Pisces—are considered the spiritual triangle of the zodiac. This gives you a head start in spiritually moving forward, and developing your philosophical and intuitive nature. Furthermore, Pluto, the planet ruling Scorpio, will transform you in the future into an incredibly perceptive and spiritually actualised individual, if you so choose.

Pisces has much to do with your past life, and you will bring in many of the intuitive and spiritual traits of this star sign.

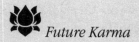

Future Karma

Your future karma is ruled by Pluto and shows that your life may be subjected to some incredible upheavals that will eventually give you the wisdom to overcome any obstacles in life.

Your most important saying or mantra is 'I Nurture'. With this statement comes your ability to help others compassionately and, in the process, empower yourself spiritually.

Mondays, Tuesdays, Thursdays and Sundays are your luckiest days for spiritual work and personal enhancement. Spend some time on these days looking into yourself and improving your personality.

Lucky Days

Your luckiest days are Monday, Tuesday, Thursday and Sunday.

Lucky Numbers

Lucky numbers for Cancer include the following. You may wish to experiment with these in lotteries and other games of chance:

2, 11, 20, 29, 38, 47

9, 18, 27, 36, 45, 54

3, 12, 21, 30, 48, 57

Destiny Years

The most significant years in your life are likely to be 2, 11, 20, 29, 38, 47, 56, 74 and 83.

HEALTH, WELLBEING ◎ AND DIET ◎

Your key zodiac element is water, which has a strong bearing not only on your emotional life but also on your health. Because of this, there is a strong link between how you feel and how well your physical body handles the stresses and strains of life, too.

Because you have a tendency to suppress your feelings, you may find that, over time, this adversely affects your physical wellbeing. Moreover, it can have an even worse effect on your health if you are not careful about eating when you are emotionally distressed. The areas of your body ruled by Cancer are the breast and stomach, as well as the circulatory and lymphatic systems.

You must always eat foods that are in keeping with your physical needs. Many Cancerians overeat, which is a problem for long-term balance. Listen to your body's signals, and you will start to enjoy a greater sense of wellbeing and health. You might try eating a greater range of fruits and vegetables—in particular, those that are useful include the lighter fruits such as bananas and melons, and vegetables such as squash and potato.

You probably enjoy dairy foods, but make them low-fat, such as cottage cheese. Consider goat's milk or low-fat milk if you like to eat and drink dairy products. Chamomile tea also has a calming influence on your intense mood swings.

◎ FINANCE FINESSE ◎

The shining Sun and the sign of Leo regulate the second zone of your horoscope, which relates to income, money and the way you view materialism as a whole. That shiny, golden, coin-like disc in the sky is all-attractive, and it represents the money that Cancerians love to have— and lots of it. It also shows you work hard to obtain it, for the purpose of security, and for feeling as comfortable as you can.

Mostly money is useful to you as a means of extending your loving nature to others. By having money you're able to uplift those who are less fortunate than yourself, and this makes you feel good.

The Sun is generally lucky and indicates you're able to earn money and put lots of energy into that process. But by the same token, money burns a hole in your pocket, and you can thank the hot Sun for that effect on your life as well.

CANCER
AT WORK

DOGS NEVER BITE ME. JUST
HUMANS.

Marilyn Monroe

CANCER CAREER

You are unable to do work that doesn't involve some component of your emotion and imagination. Emotionally divorcing yourself from your work is not possible if you're born under the star sign of Cancer. To you, work needs to be, first and foremost, an expression of your ability to care for and nourish something from inception to completion.

Attention to detail is a personality trait not often associated with you, but rather, with the sign of Virgo. However, if you look carefully, you'll see that Virgo indeed rules the third sector of the horoscope for Cancer, indicating the involvement of your mind in your day-to-day routine. So you do possess an element of fastidiousness when it comes to doing your job properly.

Jupiter

Your workplace planet is Jupiter. What does this mean to you professionally? Jupiter is the largest of the planets, and can sometimes be excessive, as well as expansive, in its action. You work hard, you work long hours, and you are prepared to put in what it takes to achieve the end result, even if it's not particularly for your own personal benefit. However, you need to ensure you don't overdo things, because, even if you are motivated by the spirit of helping family and loved ones, this very process will keep you away from them, anchoring you to your workplace.

You're primarily a responsible and punctual individual, and will therefore do your best to be fair in providing your services professionally. You must be careful not to extend yourself to helping too many people, as you may find yourself out of time for your own deadlines. It pays to be just a little selfish when it comes to your professional outlook.

 Mars

Because your career planet, Mars, rules activity and drive, you are a tireless worker. This means you need to know when to STOP! Take a break if your workload is getting the better of you.

⊚ CANCER BOSS ⊚

An employer or boss born under the sign of Cancer likes to ensure that their place of work is almost a second home. There's probably an ulterior motive behind this—if you think about it, the more comfortable you feel working in a certain environment, the more likely you are to stay there and work longer and harder. In this way, the Cancer boss can elicit the best working responses from their employees. But they truly do, at the end of the day, care for those who work under their employ.

The Cancer boss is intuitive and understanding of the needs of their workers and their industry, often without even being fed information. They always have their eyes on the ball, and can sense when to make certain strategic moves.

The interesting thing is that although Cancer is regarded as a nurturing sign, Cancerian business managers are still out to make a dollar—just not necessarily at the expense of others. They are shrewd and calculating when it comes to making money, and often his or her ability to remain silent at the right moment gives them leverage over their competitors. Hence: many successful business people are born under the sign of Cancer.

You must never assume that because the Cancer boss is overly busy that they overlook or forget things, even minor details. Wrong! The Cancer boss is as sharp as a tack—they know where every penny is being spent, and where you may be spending your loose minutes, so to speak, when you probably think they're unaware of where you're at or what you're doing.

Although their goal is to make money, sympathy and compassion are a big part of their natures. If you ever need a helping hand, your Cancer boss will be there to support you. This is because it serves two purposes: firstly, to help you; and secondly, they know that, by helping you, they will be helping their business.

A Cancerian boss is a nurturing individual and will treat you as one of the family if and when you prove to be loyal. Just as a mother looks after each and every need of her children, so too will your Cancerian boss tend to your needs if you prove to be trustworthy.

CANCER
◎ EMPLOYEE ◎

The work philosophy and ethic of a Cancerian is rather simple. You're not prone to the glitz and glamour of some of the other star signs when it comes to the reasons why you work. Security, doing a job well and serving others are more than enough to give you a strong sense of satisfaction.

Because of this, you'll make doubly sure that you don't risk losing your job by being inattentive, sloppy, or unpunctual. Nor will you take for granted the fact that you're fortunate enough to have a job. All this you do because you value a job that gives you the means of providing security for yourself and your family.

You're a dependable person, and although you're ambitious to climb the ladder of success, you may not always articulate this fact. This could be the reason why some people underestimate your power and ability to achieve great things. One day you'll prove them wrong.

Because Cancer is a cardinal, intuitive and flexible sign, many of you can—and do—take on big responsibilities and leadership roles. In saying this, I understand that each and every day is used by you as a building block to achieve your goals.

This is an excellent law of power that Cancerians use with great skill and strategy. Apart from issues of security, one of the primary motives for you to work is to serve others well and do something that has some greater meaning than the simple acquisition of power and money. Because of this, you're a genuine worker, and you will make positive contributions to your community and society through your professional endeavours.

DISCERNING (AND CALCULATING) CANCER

The Cancerian employee is very discerning when it comes to dealing with superiors. Little do they know that a charming, sympathetic and warm personality is not the only strength the Crab possesses. Behind that mask you may even be thinking of taking over their job, without them ever suspecting it in the least.

PROFESSIONAL RELATIONSHIPS: BEST AND WORST

BEST PAIRING: CANCER AND TAURUS

Although Taurus is, to a large extent, inflexible on many points of view, you and they can enjoy a professional relationship that will bring you both financial and material success and security.

Taurus, the eleventh sign to Cancer, is an earthy, practical and feminine sign, which complements your own. Although your ruling planets are not what would be considered bosom buddies astrologically speaking, there's much going for your professional and financial connection, which should be taken seriously and developed.

Given that Taurus falls in the zone of friendship and life fulfilment for you, this is an excellent combination that can meet your professional and social needs at the same time. You must, however, be cautious, not letting your intense emotional nature impinge upon the professional relationship. Although Taurus is a very earthed and reliable sign, like anyone else they have a limit to their patience, and when they explode, they really go off. You'll soon know about it.

You like the fact that Taurus is extremely hardworking, and for them you seem to exhibit a wonderful combination of sensitivity, imagination and compassion. The two of you complement each other, and can compensate for some of those areas in yourselves that are lacking.

You also like the fact that Taurus is extremely materially oriented—obviously a little more than you, but that's of no concern given that, with them, you'll be able to achieve a level of security that relieves you of the worry of providing for your family. It will create a lifestyle that, to a large extent, gives you the time to pursue other interests.

WORST PAIRING:
CANCER AND SAGITTARIUS

Sagittarius, although a very friendly sign to you, is ruled by Jupiter, which indicates that you're best to keep any involvement with them on a purely social, rather than commercial or business level.

The first reason I would dissuade you from getting involved with Sagittarius is because the element ruling their star sign is fire. This, and the fact that it falls in the sixth zone to your Sun sign, indicates they have a very different attitude to you and the way you do things and will be a drain on your finances.

Let's take the first issue: their element of fire. When we combine fire with water, your element, we see that they cancel each other out. Fire evaporates water, while water extinguishes fire. The basic qualities of your personalities will not be augmented by your association with each other.

The second issue is that your sixth zone is one of debt and enmity. What this means is that Sagittarius is extremely magnanimous, independent and sometimes less concerned about stability and security, and you might see their open-handedness as a threat to your business foundations.

STRUCTURED CANCER

You also have an interest in structuring a business in a slightly more conservative and homely fashion. Sagittarius likes to play things by ear, using a more spontaneous attitude that unsettles you considerably.

In short, this is quite an unsavoury combination that could end up causing you debts and, in the long run, a weakened relationship, if not enmity, between the two of you.

CANCER
IN LOVE

IT IS BETTER TO REMAIN QUIET AND
BE THOUGHT A FOOL.

Abraham Lincoln

ROMANTIC
⊚ COMPATIBILITY ⊚

How compatible are you with your current partner, lover or friend? Did you know that astrology can reveal a whole new level of understanding between people, simply by looking at their star sign and that of their partner? I'd like to share some special insights that will help you better appreciate your strengths and challenges using Sun sign compatibility.

The Sun reflects your drive, willpower and personality. The essential qualities of two star signs blend like two pure colours that produce an entirely new colour. Relationships, similarly, produce their own emotional colours when two people interact. The following section is a general guide to your romantic prospects with others and how, by knowing the astrological 'colour' of each other, the art of love can help you create a masterpiece.

Each of the twelve star signs has a greater or lesser affinity with the others. The two quick-reference tables will show you who's hot and who's not as far as your relationships are concerned.

The Star Sign Compatibility table rates your chance as a percentage of general compatibility, while the Horoscope Compatibility table summarises the reasons why. The results of each star sign combination are also listed.

When reading I ask you to remember that no two star signs are ever *totally* incompatible. With effort and compromise, even the most difficult astrological matches can work. Don't close your mind to the full range of life's possibilities! Learning about each other and ourselves is the most important facet of astrology.

Good luck in your search for love, and may the stars shine upon you in 2012!

STAR SIGN COMPATIBILITY
FOR LOVE AND FRIENDSHIP
(PERCENTAGES)

	Aries	Taurus	Gemini	Cancer	Leo	Virgo	Libra	Scorpio	Sagittarius	Capricorn	Aquarius	Pisces
Aries	60	65	65	65	90	45	70	80	90	50	55	65
Taurus	60	70	70	80	70	90	75	85	50	95	80	85
Gemini	70	70	75	60	80	75	90	60	75	50	90	50
Cancer	65	80	60	75	70	75	60	95	55	45	70	90
Leo	90	70	80	70	85	75	65	75	95	45	70	75
Virgo	45	90	75	75	75	70	80	85	70	95	50	70
Libra	70	75	90	60	65	80	80	85	80	85	95	50
Scorpio	80	85	60	95	75	85	85	90	80	65	60	95
Sagittarius	90	50	75	55	95	70	80	85	85	55	60	75
Capricorn	50	95	50	45	45	95	85	65	55	85	70	85
Aquarius	55	80	90	70	70	50	95	60	60	70	80	55
Pisces	65	85	50	90	75	70	50	95	75	85	55	80

In the compatibility table above please note that some compatibilities have seemingly contradictory ratings. Why you ask? Well, remember that no two people experience the relationship in exactly the same way. For one person a relationship may be more advantageous, more supportive than for the other. Sometimes one gains more than the other partner and therefore the compatibility rating will be higher for them.

HOROSCOPE COMPATIBILITY ❧ FOR CANCER ❧

Cancer with		Romance/Sexual
Aries	👎	Conflicts arise through Aries' independence and your homeliness—not an ideal match
Taurus	💘	Gentle and loving relationship; strong family ties
Gemini	👎	Mismatched emotionally and mentally, but Gemini likes your sensitivity

Friendship	Professional
✔ Challenging on most levels, they are big thinkers and can leave you reeling with their far fetched ideas	✘ You may feel obliged to serve them, working harder and harder to fulfil their needs, which could eventually wear you into the ground
✔ If you're interested in sharing ideas and listening to what they have to say, this combination could be a good match for you	✔ Taurus is generally a stable sign financially. Make sure you set clear boundaries at the very start
✔ They will be totally surprised at your uncanny ability to guess their thoughts and feelings	✔ Compromise is the key word if the two of you are going to make this combination work

Cancer with		Romance/Sexual
Cancer		Sensitive, sympathetic and emotional, but pendulum swings in their moods are a problem
Leo		Loving, warm and sexual; some differences may be overcome
Virgo		Devoted, protective and loving, but Virgo can be too critical
Libra		Peaceful and harmonious in the beginning, but could clash as time wears on

Friendship	Professional
✔ This can be a really good combination, because you will pick up each other's moods and states of mind easily	✔ On the whole, this is quite a good match and it will be improved if one of you learns to control your emotional volatility
✘ Not very compatible with you—you feel overpowered by them	✔ They are your proverbial rabbit's foot; your energies blend well, and you stimulate their ambitions
✘ You tend to be too vulnerable for their ruthless and incessant demands for perfection	✔ You respect the way you each come to conclusions over creative problems and can learn much from each other
✘ Because you want to accommodate people, you find yourself becoming victim to the worst side of their personality	✔ This partnership has some very positive things going for it, but it will also have its challenges

Cancer with		Romance/Sexual
Scorpio		Great rapport and sexually intense
Sagittarius		Very different personalities and not destined for the long run
Capricorn		Conservative combination and mutually nurturing; Capricorn can be a little cool
Aquarius		Not a great match, but worth a try if you want to take a gamble

	Friendship		Professional
✘	You need to handle the possessiveness of Scorpio and yield to the Scorpio will	✔	You can learn a lot from Scorpios—they will act as mentors to you in business and life generally
✔	There's a reasonable degree of compatibility, even if it isn't a perfect match	✔	Be prepared for lots of travel and movement if you decide to tread a professional path with them
✘	They don't always stimulate your imagination, but they are down to Earth	✔	Money doesn't take the lead role in your story of a successful professional relationship, but you're happy to have it—it is a means to an end
✘	This combination brings into play a very electric and often highly strung combination	✘	Aquarians like to be daredevils, and unpredictability is their middle name—this is not usually your cup of tea

Cancer with		Romance/Sexual
Pisces		Sensitive, receptive but also rather moody; sexually satisfying

Friendship	Professional
✔ You see each other's needs and fulfil them far better than most other star signs	✗ Success depends on your ability to lead them towards more practicality

CANCER
◎ PARTNERSHIPS ◎

Cancer + Aries

Aries has a need for independence and spontaneity, and this can be at odds with your need for warmth. But Aries can learn to be compassionate from their association with you. Those born under Cancer will learn to be more independent, and can develop resilience to criticism, by being with Aries.

Cancer + Taurus

Both of you are essentially soft and gentle people and enjoy each other's company, and also like to avoid confrontation and arguments. This will create a peaceful life for you. Your loyalty to the family unit is a common thread that helps augment your security together.

Cancer + Gemini

At times you are completely engrossed in the problems that others bring you while Gemini, your partner, is only willing to get involved to a point. While they are attracted to your emotional sensitivity, they are predominantly people who live in their minds.

Cancer + Cancer

You are both sensitive individuals with sympathy and emotion, but this affects your relationship because you are both way too moody. However, because you have empathy you do understand each other, and your intuition means you can communicate without words.

 Cancer + Leo

You have a very warm and attractive relationship with each other, even though your temperaments are at odds. Leo appreciates your warm and loving support.

 Cancer + Virgo

Both of you show a strong sense of protection towards your friends and loved ones, but temperamentally you are quite different. You should get along well together as long as Virgo is not too critical.

 Cancer + Libra

You both need people around you to feel happy in life, but prefer the harmony and peace of your own lives and individual relationships with others. As long as respect underpins your partnership, there shouldn't be too many major clashes. Libra can be a little too social for you at times.

 Cancer + Scorpio

You understand each other wonderfully, and these two water signs indicate emotional and sexual intensity. You are both great friends, but you both must guard against possessiveness and jealousy.

 Cancer + Sagittarius

Your temperaments are very different. Sagittarians are idealistic and sometimes very free and easy, while you are very emotional and at times conservative. You may overdose on each other, so small snippets of each other's company are advised.

 Cancer + Capricorn

Both of you are disinclined to take a punt on any unnecessary risk, especially when it comes to relationships. Capricorn is, however, ambitious, practical and concerned with their and your security. Mutual nurturing is part of this relationship.

Cancer + Aquarius

Once trust is established between you and Aquarius, this relationship can be quite an interesting one. Nevertheless, you are both very different, considering that progressive Aquarius is difficult to domesticate.

Cancer + Pisces

This is an excellent match because you are both sensitive, receptive and will satisfy each other's needs on every level. Pisces lives in the clouds, whereas you have your feet firmly planted on the ground. Your moods can clash.

PLATONIC RELATIONSHIPS: BEST AND WORST

BEST PAIRING: CANCER AND TAURUS

The mutual attraction between Cancer and Taurus is immediate, and if you find yourself in a social setting together, it's a foregone conclusion that you will pretty much hit it off straight away. Such is the case when a star sign falls in the eleventh place to your own, which it is with Taurus.

A solid and abiding relationship can be looked forward to once you connect with a Taurean-born character. This is because you are receptive to the needs of others, and Taurus is, in its own way, solidly anchored to your idea of security based upon tenderness, affection and material support. In addition to that, you somehow admire the solid and straightforward personality of the Bull.

You have much in common when it comes to your domestic lives. Even though socially you seem to get on well, you will probably find yourselves spending a lot of time in each other's company behind closed doors. You don't mind that, and, in fact, you both feel more comfortable and are better able to open up to each other this way.

Taurus is not particularly fazed by your changeable moods, and this can help anchor your temperament and make you a better person. By the same token, your sensitive and emotional expression helps Taurus come out of themselves and share much of what they are feeling with you. In short, this relationship is a great one, and one in which you can genuinely feel the bonds of friendship.

WORST PAIRING: CANCER AND AQUARIUS

If you and Aquarius are happy simply to shake hands and leave it at that, then that's quite alright, because astrologically speaking, that's probably as far as this friendship will go.

Although you are a caring person and sensitive to the needs of others, you do so in a way that is not entirely obvious. You could feel jaded by the Aquarian tendency to go about improving everything and everyone, almost to the extent of fanaticism. Yes, you both are motivated by similar things, but the way in which you go about them is very, very different.

The Cancer-born individual has a wonderful knack of intuiting things, and this is based on having a deep, emotional sensitivity. Aquarius is proud, if not arrogant, of the intellectual prowess they possess. And they certainly do have a fine mind, with a broad-based view of most things. But these two temperamental aspects of your star signs are diametrically opposed, and in the long term, there will be conflicts, no doubt about that.

When it comes to socialising, Aquarius needs to be out and about, discovering new things and people, and revolutionising that which is not new. You are quite content to entertain at home, keep to yourself, and even if you do go out for dinner in a social context, you prefer a much more low-key environment. Here again, we see the very different attitudes of Cancer and Aquarius that make this a pretty untenable friendship over the long haul.

CANCER AND AQUARIUS: HOMEY MEETS HIPPIE

A passionate, if not spasmodic, sexual relationship is likely between the two of you. The Aquarian's hippie approach to sex is a little too way out in your view, and will not fulfil you. But at least you will have a few fireworks!

Aquarius will leave you up in the air about where you stand, particularly in relation to the emotional status quo. And can you tie them down? Absolutely not! Still, if you're prepared to venture forth and explore life with an Aquarian, you may have many exhilarating adventures.

SEXUAL RELATIONSHIPS:
BEST AND WORST

BEST PAIRING:
CANCER AND SCORPIO

Scorpio falls in the fifth sign from Cancer, it's of the same element, and it has a planet extremely friendly to your own. These three things make this match an excellent one.

There is an instantaneous emotional and physical attraction between the two of you. Although, don't for a minute think that you won't have your challenges.

I often chuckle when people ask me whether or not they have met their soulmate because initially they may be having some problems. I tell them that, even in the most perfect of relationships, such challenges are there as a means of helping you grow. The Cancer-Scorpio sexual match is no different.

The two of you have an abundant amount of emotional wealth to share with each other, and also love your sexual connection, which is based on emotionalism. On every level this match does seem to fit the ideal.

Cancer, you'll feel that you're destined to be with Scorpio, but their responses will never seem to be enough. You'll want more and more and more.

One aspect of this relationship that needs to be carefully monitored is that you are both such deep-feeling people that your moods will often clash. On the one hand, this is not a great thing, because you can spend chunks of time not talking to each other and brooding. But on the other hand, the advantage is that you get to kiss and make up, and when we talk of sex, we talk of the opportunity to reciprocate and make things better. The two of you will do this very well by having an innate sense of each other's needs.

Scorpio needs the affectionate warmth and demonstrativeness of you, Cancer. Even though they have loads of passion to give, Scorpio is secretive, and sometimes prefers to play the power game of withholding. You, and perhaps only Pisces, may be in a position to know just how to deal with this rather enigmatic personality trait of your Scorpio lover.

You probably handle the possessiveness of Scorpio better than most signs, because you are an adaptable sign and can comfortably adjust to the Scorpio will. But Scorpio has to learn to control their desires to dominate and push people away through their sometimes unrealistic demands, both practical and emotional. Scorpio will use power, on any level, to get what they want.

Although Cancer and Scorpio are elementally well suited, both being water signs, there are differences sexually. Scorpio is driven by the purely sensual. You, Cancer, need love and bonding, not just raw sex. This match is, nevertheless, one destined to last, and encapsulates all of the best elements of friendship, love and sex.

WORST PAIRING:
CANCER AND LIBRA

There is an obstacle at the outset with the Cancer-Libra combination, and strangely, you may be drawn to giving it a go, despite yourselves. Although Libra is sensitive and, at times, very passionate, their response to life is primarily through their minds and verbal communication. And you know very well that the Cancerian view of life is based on your feelings, emotional responses and intuitive understanding of things. That's why the two of you may never see eye to eye, and even if you enjoy physical intimacy together for a while, you will both always feel as if something is lacking, that you don't quite connect on the deepest level.

Some Cancerians (even if others don't tell you so) are quite possessive of their partners. If, for some reason, you are reading this and you are already involved with a Libran, you will need to sort out that aspect of your relationship quick smart. Libra will not put up with such possessiveness and, being the social butterflies that they are, they won't be hanging around for too long. If you want to win the heart and body of Libra, you need to give them sufficient independence and, likewise, express your own self-confidence, so that you don't come across as too needy.

Unfortunatel,y the Cancerian need for stable domestic security will not meet the Libran need for social and creative variety, especially in the earlier part of life. Maybe later on you can give this combination a go, but the general assessment of it is not at all promising.

Coming to a firm decision is not one of Libra's best attributes. You, on the other hand, have a strong sense of prudence and economy. You can manage a house and budgets quite well.

The significant differences between you reveal themselves over time, when Cancer's need for a quiet and peaceful domestic life comes up against the Libran's social, playful and variety-seeking nature. Libra may see you as a stick in the mud; they need a wider group of people with whom to share their social life.

The intimacy match of Libra and Cancer is not always great, even though the Moon and Venus rule both these signs. You both love to be loved and to give love, so you both need to feel nurtured and appreciated sexually. Are you up to the task? Maybe not.

QUIZ:
HAVE YOU FOUND YOUR PERFECT
◉ MATCH? ◉

Do you dare take the following quiz to see just how good a lover you are? Remember, although the truth sometimes hurts, it's the only way to develop your relationship skills.

We are all searching for our soulmate: that idyllic romantic partner who will fulfil our wildest dreams of love and emotional security. Unfortunately, finding true love isn't easy. Sometimes, even when you are in a relationship, you can't help but wonder whether or not your partner is right for you. How can you possibly know?

It's essential to question your relationships and to work on ways that will improve your communication and overall happiness with your partner. It's also a good idea, when meeting someone new, to study their intentions and read between the lines. In the first instance, when your hormones are taking over, it's easy to get carried away and forget some of the basic principles of what makes for a great relationship that is going to endure.

You're probably wondering where to start. Are you in a relationship currently? Are you looking for love, but finding it difficult to choose between two or more people? Are you simply not able to meet someone? Well, there are some basic questions you can ask yourself to discover the truth of just how well suited you and your partner are for each other. If you don't have a partner at the moment, you might like to reflect on your previous relationships to improve your chances next time round.

The following quiz is a serious attempt to take an honest look at yourself and see whether or not your relationships are on track. Don't rush through the questionnaire, but think carefully about your practical day-to-day life and whether or not the relationship you are in genuinely fulfils your needs and the other person's needs. There's no point being in a relationship if you're gaining no satisfaction out of it.

Now, if you aren't completely satisfied with the results you get, don't give up! It's an opportunity for you to work at the relationship and to improve things. But you mustn't let your ego get in the road, because that's not going to get you anywhere.

As a Cancer, you're in tune with passion and emotion, and need someone to nurture you to the maximum. You need a partner who can understand the changes in your moods from moment to moment. There are some unique requirements that you need to be happy in your romantic life. So here's a checklist for you, Cancer, to see if he or she's the right partner for you.

Scoring System:

Yes = 1 point

No = 0 points

- ❓ Do his or her family and your family both approve of your relationship?

- ❓ Does he or she take you to good restaurants and provide you with a great food?

- ❓ Does he or she compliment and appreciate you?

- ❓ Is he or she sensitive to your needs?

- ❓ Does he or she help you overcome your insecurities and fears?

- ❓ Does he or she devote loving time to you?

- ❓ Does he or she provide you a shoulder to cry on when you need it most?

- ❓ Does he or she make you feel stable and protected?

- ❓ Do you feel safe around him or her?

- ❓ Do you completely trust him or her?

- ❓ Does he or she provide you with constant reassurance of their love for you?

- ❓ Is he or she able to tune into your moods without you saying anything?

- ❓ Is he or she ready for a commitment, like someone who is up for a marriage and family?

- ❓ Is he or she honest and sincere with you?

❷ Does he or she feel comfortable enough with you to reveal their inner secrets?

❷ Is he or she a Scorpio, Pisces, Virgo, Cancer or Taurus?

Have you jotted down your answers honestly? If you're finding it hard to come up with the correct answers, let your intuition help and try not to force them. Of course, there's no point pretending and turning a blind eye to treatment that is less than acceptable, otherwise you're not going to have a realistic appraisal of your prospects with your current love interest. Here are the possible points you can score.

8 to 16 points

A good match. This shows you've obviously done something right, and that the partner you have understands you and is able to reciprocate in just the way you need. But this doesn't mean you should become lazy and not continue working on your relationship. There's always room to improve and make your already excellent relationship even better.

5 to 7 points

Half-hearted prospect. You're going to need to work hard at your relationship, and this will require a close self-examination of just who may be at fault. You know, it takes two to tango, and it's more than likely a combination of both your attitudes is what is dragging down your relationship. Systematically go over each of the above questions and try to make a list of where you can improve. I guarantee that your relationship will improve if given some time and sincerity on your part. If, after a genuine effort of working at it, you find things still haven't improved, it may be time for you to rethink your future with this person.

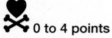 **0 to 4 points**

On the rocks. I'm sorry to say that this relationship is not founded on a sufficiently strong enough base of mutual respect and understanding. It's likely that the two of you argue a lot, don't see eye to eye or, frankly, have completely different ideas of what sort of lifestyle and emotional needs you each have. The big question here is why are you still with this person?

Again, this requires some honest self-examination to see if there is some inherent insecurity which is causing you to hold on to something that has outgrown its use in your life. Old habits die hard, as they say, and you may also fear letting go of a relationship that you have become accustomed to, even though it doesn't fulfil your needs. Self-honesty is the key here. At certain times in life you may need to make some rather big sacrifices to move on to a new phase, which will then hopefully attract the right sort of partner to you.

2012
YEARLY OVERVIEW

WE NEVER SHALL HAVE ANY MORE
TIME. WE HAVE, AND WE HAVE
ALWAYS HAD, ALL THE TIME THERE
IS.

Thomas A. Bennett

⊚ KEY EXPERIENCES ⊚

Saturn moves out of your zone of family and home during 2012—in October. This will be a welcome relief for you, after enduring a couple of years of intense responsibility centring on certain delicate, older members of the family. Up until that time, however, you may still have to shoulder some difficult responsibilities, but you'll breathe a sigh of relief afterwards.

The other two significant transits include the influence of Jupiter on your social activities. It impacts on 2012 by making it a year for excellent social networking, and an accumulation of new and beneficial friends. Neptune transits to your zone of spirituality, higher learning and foreign journeys, and after the end of February, a dream you've cherished in one of these areas may come to pass.

ROMANCE AND
⊚ FRIENDSHIP ⊚

There are some key dates to be aware of in 2012, and around these times, relationships will come into focus for you.

In particular, Mars will be an important planet for you during the coming twelve months, while Venus has a large part to play in the development of your personal affairs.

On the 11th of January, Venus influences your sexuality in a highly significant way. You may experience more love and attention from your partner or spouse. The 26th highlights this same thing, and makes you feel confident about your relationships.

Romantic opportunities surface when Venus transits your social zone after the 31st of March. In fact, the period throughout March and April brings you in contact with many potential lovers, or at least good friends, if you're not feeling that way inclined.

August is an incredibly important month, with both Venus and Mars influencing your life in a big way. Mars enters your zone of love affairs on the 23rd, with Venus just behind it, entering the Sun sign on the 7th of September. You'll be shining and others will notice. You have perfect timing to make your presence felt in any social situation where romance is on offer.

Mars also becomes powerful again around October, especially after the 2nd. However, you will have some problems—perhaps a power play or issues regarding jealousy and past secrets—at this time. By the 21st of November, when Venus enters Scorpio, you should be able to reconcile these issues and enjoy your personal affairs much more.

YOU FEEL GREAT ABOUT YOURSELF

The placement of Venus in your Sun sign in May indicates an excellent period for you to take your image and change it into something newer, fresher and more appealing. Now would be the perfect opportunity for you to revamp your wardrobe, get a manicure, a facial, or change the colour of your hair. You will certainly be attractive to members of the opposite sex.

Marriage, long-term commitment and deep feelings of connectedness with someone are hinted at by the entry of Mars into Capricorn around the 16th of November. This period makes you very proactive, and up until Christmas Day, the 25th of December, when Mars enters Aquarius, this should be a prime time for you to enjoy love and romance.

Relationships on the Rise

There are some additional times and dates which are important to write in your diary if you are to enjoy 2012 and fully maximise the opportunities present. You can put your best foot forward romantically when Venus enters Aries around the 8th of February. Your workplace will be buzzing with social activities, and an opportunity to meet somebody at this time is on the cards.

The 21st of February indicates a time when you may be out of sync with others and feel uncomfortable in the company of the people you are with. Try to step aside, and don't force yourself to be everything to all people.

Social opportunities are big after the 31st of March, but there may be some problems trying to balance your loyalties between your social activities and your more personal and committed relationships. Money may be an issue at this time, so communication will be important to level the playing field, and not feel as if you're being pressured.

Time aside—that is, some quiet time with the one you love—should take precedence over everything else throughout April. It's a good time to get away and consolidate your feelings with the person special to you.

Arguments are likely throughout the early part of August, but by the 23rd, Mars gives you the tenacity and determination to make things work. By September the 9th, Saturn will exert its influence on your sexual affairs through the eighth and twelfth zones of your horoscope. There could be a cooling off of your feelings. There are other matters possibly distracting you, your partner or friends as well, which make it hard for you to connect. By the 16th, Mars, in its prime to the Sun indicates a smoothing over of these problems, but you have to take the bull by its horns, so to speak, and be the hero in this situation.

With Saturn entering Scorpio on October 5th, a serious period in your relationships is likely to occur, and this will not be a short cycle. In fact, Saturn could affect you in the realm of romance, creativity and affairs of youngsters for two to two-and-half years. You'll become much more serious about your relationships, and this could become more pronounced by November and early December, when Venus combines with Saturn, creating a need to renovate your relationships.

WORK AND MONEY

Harness Your Moneymaking Powers

Making money can be summed up in an equation:

$$m \text{ (\$ money)} = e \text{ (energy)} \times t \text{ (time)} \times l \text{ (love)}$$

If one of the above factors is not present—for example, energy or love—you could still make money, but you won't be ideally fulfilled in the process.

It's absolutely essential to understand the universal laws of attraction and success when speaking about money. It is also necessary to understand that when you love what you do, you infuse your work with the qualities of attention, love and perfection.

With these qualities, you endow your work with a sort of electromagnetic appeal: a power that draws people to your work and causes them to appreciate what you do. This, in turn, generates a desire for people to use your services, buy your products and respect you for the great work you perform. This will without a doubt elevate you to higher and higher positions because you will be regarded as someone who exercises great diligence and skill in your actions.

To understand your capacity to earn money fully, we need to look at the Sun's movement in your horoscope, particularly throughout 2012. Because it is found closely conjoined to Pluto in your zone of business partnerships, you should focus your attention on this area, and 2012 will bring you benefits associated with this.

The planet of profit for Cancer is Venus, which is also associated with other people's money throughout 2012. Especially in the first month of the year, you should do everything you can to put forward your good ideas, and to elicit a favourable response with the promise of investment loans or other financial supports for your concepts and business ideas.

Some particularly strong dates on which to focus your moneymaking powers are, for example, when Venus enters Taurus on the 5th of March, when you have the opportunity to combine your efforts with those of friends or co-workers and really do something magnificent. The Sun accentuates this after the 19th of April, so this whole period should be one where team effort should take precedence over your personal efforts. The key phrase for you to remember at this time is: 'No one is an island unto themselves'.

Speculative affairs, and using your imagination to improve your financial circumstances, can take place when Venus, the Sun and Mars come to your fifth zone of speculation and creative activities. This will happen in the latter part of August, and indicates that your industriousness is paying off. Contracts at this time, and all through September, are powerfully indicated by the conjoined energies of Mercury and the Sun in your third zone. Use communication to your best advantage during this cycle.

BUCKET-WITH-HOLES CYCLE

You may have some difficulties after the 11th of January, due to the influence of Venus in your zone of expenses, insurances, loans and other people's money. You may need to pay back some debt quickly, or work through other measures to get on top of things. Your financial worth is like a bucket at the moment: are there holes in it, draining your bank balance?

With the Sun entering Scorpio around the 24th of October, and Venus entering the same sign in November, the last two or three months of your year should, once again, be solidly concentrated on developing your creative ideas. Sometimes we are afraid to reveal these ideas, because we might be embarrassed of what others think. This is no time to shrink back and let these doubts dominate you. The last two months of the year are indeed an excellent time for you to enjoy the success of your hard work.

You mustn't be concerned that, after October, Saturn will be influencing this zone of creativity. What this will do is simply make you more cautious and grounded in developing these ideas. The perfect balance of practicality, idealism and hard work is what is indicated for helping you really make the most of your moneymaking skills.

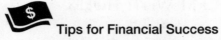 **Tips for Financial Success**

It's important to have your diary out, so you can mark some of the key times throughout the coming year when you can capitalise upon financial opportunities.

Let's take a look at the Sun, and its movement through your horoscope, to see when and how you can extract money from the situations that arise, shall we?

A contract may be on offer after the 17th of January. The Sun combines with Mars, meaning you shouldn't get involved in any arguments, but use diplomacy to get what you want.

Legal matters after the 19th need to be addressed and not swept under the rug if you are to achieve a rock-solid result in 2012. Do what needs to be done, and consult the professionals if you are in doubt.

You need to look to mentoring to help you develop your skills throughout 2012. An opportunity for this presents itself after the 19th of April, when the Sun transits Taurus. Don't be afraid to ask for help and learn from the experts.

Don't spend up too big when the Sun enters your finance sector after the 22nd of July. Save a little bit, and don't be embarrassed about bargain hunting.

Believe it or not, you need to work on yourself throughout August. The reason I say this is that the combined influence of Mars and Saturn can make things very frustrating for you. If you are too emotionally involved in problems, you are going to miss many opportunities, and this will be the case throughout the whole month of August. Try to set aside your personal problems and focus on the work at hand.

As I said earlier, the period of September, October and November is powerful for employing your imaginative skills in your work activities. This is the time of the year when your ideas will be received well by others.

Finally, in December, just when Neptune enters your zone of higher learning, it's not a bad idea to book yourself into a course of study to further enhance your skills, and help you earn much more money in the future.

 Career Moves and Promotions

Mars is predominantly your best planet for career, and has a strong impact upon your life throughout the coming year. However, between January and July, you may find yourself stuck in a rut, or frustrated in being unable to move things forward.

That obstruction to your career may finally start to move after July, when Mars influences both your career sector and the planet Uranus, which is transiting your career sector. Some time in the latter part of July, a sudden opportunity may arise and you should seize the moment to push forward your career aspirations. Yet again, Mars and Saturn may obstruct you, but it's a good time to commence things, as long as you're patient and don't expect things to happen too quickly.

NEGOTIATION HOT SPOT

The transit of Mars through your sixth zone of work through October and November is an opportune time to make some moves to advance yourself professionally. However, be careful of those who may be envious of you.

In the latter part of November and December, you have the green light to ask for a pay rise or, indeed, a promotion. For those of you adventurous enough, it could be time to move on and take up a job in a completely new industry or area.

 When to Avoid Office Politics

Office politics seem to be part and parcel of work these days, so it's good to know when antagonistic, stressful days are going to ruffle your feathers.

It's essential to sidestep any problems associated with work, especially if it involves politics and those who may undermine your best efforts to achieve success in your chosen vocation. For this reason, let's look at the important transits of Jupiter and Mars, to establish when problems are likely.

Fortunately, this year Jupiter transits your zone of friendships after the 29th of May, but prior to that, some problems may result from getting your boss or co-workers offside. Try to be more diplomatic and don't say too much.

Worse than enemies you are able to see, hear and do battle with, are those who are less conspicuous. These are your secret enemies, and there are indications that when Jupiter transits your hidden zone of Gemini after the 11th of June, you may feel that things are on the mend. But be careful—the knives may be out and you might not even be aware of it. These secret enemies may undermine you through malicious gossip and other tactics designed to cut you down.

When Mars enters your sixth zone of workplace activities, you may discover who some of these enemies are, and it could surprise you. This may happen soon after the last week of October, with Mars's influence continuing up until the latter part of November. You may be able to confront those individuals after the first week of December.

HEALTH, BEAUTY AND
⊚ LIFESTYLE ⊚

 Venus Calendar for Beauty

There are some wonderful opportunities to show off your best self throughout 2012, Cancer. Let's look at the movement of Venus to see how it most positively impacts you, and, of course, when the best times are to attract others, particularly members of the opposite sex.

The triangular position of Venus to the Sun on the 26th of January indicates that your personality will be bubbly, warm and attractive at that time. Use these energies to make an impact in any sort of social engagement.

When Venus enters Taurus on the 5th of March, you may have the opportunity to meet many friends, but don't be slack in applying makeup, paying more attention to colour combinations, and polishing up on your etiquette. Just because you are meeting people doesn't mean they are all going to be totally impressed by you. Go the extra mile to win over a few extra hearts. Between the 19th and the 25th, the Sun makes its entry into your zone of social activities which should be a continuation of the energy I just mentioned.

If you are trying to make inroads into new relationships—a new partnership, for example—there are some beautiful, sweet planetary energies around on the 7th of August, when Venus enters your Sun sign. These energies continue to get stronger; in particular, there will be some perfect opportunities not only to mend current relationships and friendships, but to develop and forge new associations after the 25th, when Venus finds your zone of friendships. Something lucky may happen to you, and you may not be aware of what you've done to invite it.

ECLIPSE HIGHLIGHT

The eclipse on the 14th of November occurs in your zone of romance. Looking your best gives you the chance to take charge of changes that occur in your relationships. You will also learn much about yourself and someone else.

This area of the horoscope—in the later part of the year—also relates to your health and vitality. It's important you pay special attention to feeding your body, in particular your nerves. Being a water sign, you are likely to struggle emotionally with some aspects of your life, and this can make you very edgy. This will require a re-evaluation of your closest relationships.

 Showing off Your Cancer Traits

Each zodiac sign has its own unique power based on the elements and planets that rule it. Unfortunately, most people don't know how to tap into this power and bring out their greatest potential to achieve success in life.

You can afford to be a little more daring and aggressive in showing off your Cancer traits this year. What I mean by this is that you shouldn't be shy in expressing your compassionate and loving ways, even if, at times, you have a sense that others are not amenable to you giving them a hand, showing them affection, and so forth.

Mars spends considerable time in your zone of communications and courage this year, and, in fact, doesn't make an exit until after July. This means the moveable traits of your sign will make you restless: perhaps you'll have the travel bug, or step up your ability to communicate your deeper feelings. You should certainly do so, and not feel embarrassed about it. In January, February and March, take the time to share your feelings with loved ones.

The movement of the Sun through critical parts of your horoscope means that others, especially in January, will welcome your need to both connect with them, and let them know exactly who you are. When the Sun hits the highest point of your horoscope in April, you'll feel appreciated, and may even achieve considerable accolades for your work or, if you're a homemaker, for the skill and attention you apply to loving and caring for those in your closest family and social circles.

Mars makes an important contact with Scorpio, which will activate your Cancerian traits and bring out a very powerful creative urge in you. Actually, this will commence from August the 23rd, and you'll feel its influence throughout the rest of the year. Let others see the dynamic side of your Cancerian personality.

SOFTER SIDE COMES OUT

Throughout August, you have a prime interval (with Venus moving through your Sun sign) to exhibit the softer side of your nature. You can blend the energies of Venus and the Moon to entertain, care for and socialise with others, perhaps even on a humanitarian or social welfare basis. You can help others while having a good time.

Best Ways to Celebrate

This year gives you the chance to explore different avenues in life, Cancer. When Venus and Jupiter transit your zone of hidden activities, around July, you'll find yourself drawn towards celebrating life in many unusual ways.

In September, Venus casts a beneficial glance on the area of your horoscope that indicates pleasure, entertainment and fun. With Mars also transiting this area, would you believe that fighting sports—hard-nosed activities such as wrestling, boxing and Thai kickboxing—might be forms of entertainment that will stimulate you? Car races and horse races will also allow you to enjoy yourself with friends and really let your hair down.

After the 26th of October there are some opportunities

for you to travel, but make them local journeys and don't pressure yourself with too much activity. You'll be surprised with just how much fun you can have in your local environment.

KARMIC FLAVOUR

You can travel this year, so explore cultures, and even spiritual philosophies, that previously have been inaccessible to you. There is a strong karmic flavour to your celebratory energy, so keep an open mind, especially after October.

KARMA, SPIRITUALITY AND EMOTIONAL ⊚ BALANCE ⊚

The planets most influencing your spirituality and karma are Jupiter, Mars and Neptune. These three planets can point the way to best developing yourself spiritually and enjoying peace of mind during 2012, Cancer.

Neptune will spend a great deal of time over the coming year in your zone of spirituality and higher mind. This indicates that you are receptive and open to some of the spiritual energies that are coming through now. Hasten that process by meditating, as well as actively inquiring into your nature and how you can best understand others. This will give you a sense of power and self-control. Of course, your relationships will improve as well.

Finally, Jupiter spends much of the year in your twelfth zone of inner reflection, charitable work and the uncovering of secrets. You will spend a great deal of time unearthing past habits that you may not have been aware of, but which can help you become much luckier in the coming twelve months.

HIGHER THOUGHT

Mars makes important transits during September,
influencing Neptune in the zone of higher thought.
This means that rather than just thinking about
spirituality, you will get active and make things
happen.

In December, Mercury, Venus and Saturn transit your fifth zone of spiritual initiation. You may have the opportunity to reach someone or some people who can reintroduce you to those parts of your character that are spiritually active. You will have some deep and long-term insights during this interval.

2012
MONTHLY & DAILY PREDICTIONS

IT IS DIFFICULT TO SAY WHO DO
YOU THE MOST HARM: ENEMIES
WITH THE WORST INTENTIONS, OR
FRIENDS WITH THE BEST.

Edward Bulwer-Lytton

❁ JANUARY ❁

 Monthly Highlight

The combined influence of the Sun and Pluto will have an intense effect on your personal relationships and marriage this month—that is, if you happen to be significantly committed. You mustn't let your emotions get the better of you. Power plays are likely, and you need to counteract these with a gentle approach. Your sexual needs may not be met to your satisfaction.

1 This is an electric sort of day, especially if you are working. Don't let your mind turn to mud, though, by doing too many things. Ideas come hard and fast.

2 Be objective about your honest and steady effort to be a good friend—you may be overdoing it. Try to create space in your relationships so you can receive as well as give.

3 You find it's worthwhile living, but only if your health is in tip-top condition. You may need to revisit some of your dietary and lifestyle patterns to improve your health.

4   You may be perpetually accommodating others and pardoning them for behaviour that demeans you. Someone may be taking advantage of you and you are overlooking it.

5   Don't let someone play a crude joke on you today—or tell jokes that bother you. Speak up if you feel uncomfortable.

6   You need to recreate the hypothetical. By this I mean that, if you first have a vision of yourself, then you can start to live up to it. Just now your self-image may be a little scrambled. Put the pieces together properly to create a better version of you.

7   If talking money, you need to be coherent, especially if trying to perfect your finances. You certainly have the benefits of Jupiter in terms of earning, but are you saving enough for the proverbial rainy day?

8   You will find a fitting solution to your problem only by listening carefully to what others have to say. You have been distracted, but you will need to put some time and energy into solving these issues yourself.

9 There could be some upsets due to the involvement of Mars. There is a resolution that you are incapable of reaching today, which is driving you completely mad. If it is out of your control, just let it be for a while.

10 You could be left baffled if you are the originator of a concept and the prize for good work goes to someone else. Once again, you need to assert yourself and take credit for all the work you have done.

11 You need to exploit possibilities today, especially those of a romantic nature. Don't be scared to step outside the square and discover new things.

12 You are a crack organiser in the workplace at the moment, and others will note your efficient ways of dealing with things. It could be that you are preparing to take on a leadership role...is that right?

13 If you allow someone to exploit you, to take advantage of your good nature and expertise, then you have only yourself to blame. This situation will require a little more awareness on your part to short-circuit a potentially uncomfortable scenario.

14 Transport issues could take on epic proportions just now, and this has to do with a lack of preparation or planning. Plan for your journey a few days ahead, even it's a small one.

15 A little chocolate goes a long way, especially if you are feeling down over some relationship or friendship. The important thing to remember is not to eat the guilt while you are eating the chocolate.

16 A disappointing accusation could leave you riddled with doubts about a friendship. It may be subtle or hidden aspects of another person's personality that trigger these feelings.

17 Even if you are dripping with profits, you may have to reassure someone that the way you are managing your money is quite acceptable. Issues of mistrust may need to be dealt with.

18 Take a realistic approach to things such as travel, journeys and holidays at the moment. You may be hoping for time away, but your schedule doesn't really allow it.

19 You need to be concentrated today, but also moderate in the way you handle your work projects. Balance is required, which will help keep your identity intact. Don't get carried off by the masses.

20 Someone you know who is unemployed may appeal to you, and you could feel wounded by their situation. You may feel you don't deserve to be where you are, but that's not going to help them.

21 Today, you might be surprised to find that your lover or partner consents to something for which you have been asking for some time. Enjoy the moment thoroughly.

22 It's pretty upsetting when someone continues to fail in their commitment. If that's happening, now is the time to take decisive action to stop it and, if necessary, step away from the situation.

23 You need to isolate your purpose if you are to achieve your ambitions. Public relations and social activities may be confusing you about what you want. Spend a little time each day re-evaluating your path.

24 Be moderate in your affection and physical appetites today. Discomfort follows excess.

25 You have the utmost intentions to meet someone and discuss financial ideas, only to find out that you are snagged by a timetable. You may need to reschedule.

26 It's wonderful how time helps to dim regrets. Some problems you had in the past may now be diminishing, much to your satisfaction.

27 Wisdom can sometimes appear quite ludicrous. You mustn't dismiss the words of a friend or a stranger today, even if they sound a little weird. There could be quite a lesson in what you hear.

28 Sidestepping mainstream ideas may not be the way to go at present, even if you wish to seem original. There is something of use even in conservative thoughts.

29 Your capabilities are conflicting with those of someone else, perhaps even a superior. Humble yourself: listen and learn.

30 You need to be guided by your intuition before paying for something. There is no harm in buying the item you desire, but you may end up paying a little too much.

31 Peering over the horizon allows you to see what's coming. I'm not necessarily talking about astrology, but now's a good time to study certain trends and facets of life to develop your own intuition.

⊚ FEBRUARY ⊚

 Monthly Highlight

You could feel as if a problem on the home front is now over, but might be surprised to learn that there are still loose ends that need to be dealt with. This could take several more months to sort out.

Friendships are on the rise, and you might now meet someone who could have a strong impact on your life. Work and pleasure seem to be linked.

1 We are all ageing, so don't worry about it. But you may be seeking juvenile outlets to avoid the fact. To some extent this is good, although it shouldn't simply be a reaction, but rather, a creative impulse to seek your inner self.

2 The human collective is sometimes an unoriginal stereotype. If you are modelling your life on these flimsy foundations, you will fail. Find your own truth.

3   If your family or peer group is making an insane fuss over something you find trivial today, then get away, disappear, and don't tell anybody where you are going. Yes, sanity once again.

4   Pride is permissible, as long as your ego doesn't stomp on others'. Enjoy making yourself up, showing off your best talents, and sharing some of the good things you have with others.

5   There could be some jealousy surrounding you at present, probably because you are approaching life in a slightly more trendy way than usual, and this is disliked by others. Who cares?

6   Some financial matter may have stalled. Now is the time to relaunch it with greater excitement, due to the fullness of the Moon in your financial zone.

7   You may be pregnant with anger, so to speak, and unable to express it after being refused either a refund or a legitimate discount on an item. You will need to find an outlet for this energy.

8   Say farewell to trash. Have a garage sale or at least somehow clear the decks to make space for new things to come into your life.

9 You may be too charitable, believing that someone's promise is forthcoming. Beware the flatterer—she or he may be feeding you with an empty spoon.

10 You need to be cunning in your work or with some simple ideas today, perhaps by coding concepts before sharing them. People love to appropriate others' hard work.

11 By understanding your family more, you will optimise your life. Don't ignore calls for some heart-to-heart communication today.

12 Your thinking is dreadful right now, and that could be causing you to react poorly to those you love most. Try to be nicer when dealing with others, even in confrontational situations.

13 There is a giant turnaround likely today, and it will be favourable for all concerned. This relates specifically to a situation that has been in stalemate.

14 There really is no use crying over a severed bond if all the while you knew the personalities involved were so dissimilar. Try to see things as they really are.

15 Today's message is to tackle the overview before you get bogged down in the detail. On another front, you may be awaiting funds that are delayed.

16 Don't jump to conclusions, especially if you previously glossed over your voicemails or messages. You may misunderstand someone's correspondence.

17 Due to cultural pressure, you could be obliged to worship in a fashion that is displeasing to you. However, it may be unavoidable.

18 Some of your admirable statements today will help stave off a fight. You don't have to suck up to someone—simply recognising their good points rather than their bad is advisable.

19 Why not wait for a friendly cue before speaking? In this way you will win someone over.

20 Today, you will find yourself throwing someone an off-handed psychological blast when they say something out of turn. You have had enough, and it's time to put them in their place.

21 If you are in a management position, your day may be spent managing and screening underlings. You have to accept the fact that if you get the bigger pay packet, dealing with this sort of stuff comes with the territory.

22 Be careful of inside practices, that is, certain activities and behaviours that have become part of your culture, and which may not be altogether right. Trust your conscience.

23 You most certainly need to modify your practices and methodologies, and also your teaching style if you are in a position to show the way to others. This will mend your broken crown if you have fallen out of favour with someone.

24 Stop focusing on extraneous items—you could be passing judgement on things that are irrelevant. Focus on the core issues.

25 Corruption and cutting corners may help achieve something quickly, but this may not be a positive outcome. An erosion of your spirit is not worth the temporary gain.

26 You will need to disguise your pleasure to deal with someone who is a little cagey today. Remember to study the non-verbal signals.

27 Strangely, you may need to use a counter-example to set a first example for someone else today. A mature task requires a lateral solution.

28 Abbreviation is the key word for you right now. Saying too much will ruin your position of power. But don't for a minute think that avoiding a discussion is going to make the other person forget, either. They won't.

29 Don't throw good money after bad during this transit. You may feel that something is a spectacular opportunity, only to realise later that your impulses were getting the better of you.

☙ MARCH ☙

Monthly Highlight

You're feeling somewhat withdrawn this month, and the difficult aspect of the Moon and Mars at the outset means you won't be able to communicate how you're feeling to anyone and may even find it difficult to figure out exactly what's bothering you. Meditation and other forms of self-reflection may help identify these issues.

Your social networking continues to be strong, with the combined influence of Venus and Jupiter giving you a great deal of hope regarding the way your friends respond to you.

1 You won't be bothered with protocol today and will prefer your own company. So be it.

2 Your collaboration with someone on a project or creative pursuit should not be so abstract. Define the parameters.

3 Issues of hiring, eliminating or commissioning new people are part of the mix of work or services around the home today. Choose well.

4   If your prospects seem limited just now, you must not project this around you. Look primarily to yourself as the cause.

5   Exhibiting *bad manners* is like putting up *mad banners*, showing everyone just how little sensitivity you have for those around you at the moment. Why not brush up on your etiquette?

6   Wise financial alterations are not easy to make at the best of times, but right now they're imperative. Reappraise your strategy.

7   A stiff bigot may damage your day. Try to remain flexible when discussing religion or politics with inflexible fanatics.

8   Even if you're accustomed to a certain amount of freedom in the way you do things, adopting textbook practices can sometimes expand your understanding and deliver practical outcomes. Remain open.

9   You hate enforced restrictions, but if your desire is to get out, you may find yourself unable to do so.

10 You can derive more benefits from your home environment today than from social activities. Catch a bit of peace and quiet, and take the phone off the hook.

11 There could be a distorted estimation about the value of work on your home just now. It may be wise to wait—or at least get several quotes—before committing.

12 Ringing your favourite friend may be a great idea today. You both have lots to talk about and, coincidentally, similar issues are arising in your lives right now.

13 Romance is on the cards at the moment, so be open to life's possibilities, even if the person you meet is, initially, not quite your cup of tea.

14 Avoid panic if you need to rectify a plan on the spur of the moment. Take a few deep breaths, and work through it systematically.

15 Project your nature and your ability to work with others favourably. Be visible, because there may be someone of note around who can help your cause.

16 An electric date will shock you in the nicest of ways today. An unexpected outcome with a member of the opposite sex encourages further opportunities.

17 A quiz is the way to relax today. Crosswords, sudoku and other mental games will happily distract you from the cares of the world.

18 There is an expansion of your awareness which may arise through a conflict with someone you love. You may realise you haven't seen a scenario for what it is. Now there's a change.

19 You will be a wizard at limiting the high maintenance of someone today. You needn't put up with the demands of people who give little in return.

20 You may end up scratching your head over a consultation—possibly medical, or even legal—and confounded by the outcome. Seek clarification before you walk out the door.

21 Don't allow your perception to continue that an injured universe is justification for your present victim mentality. Take responsibility for your thoughts, words and actions.

22   There are passionate indications in the heavens just now, but you must exercise good judgement. Don't do anything you will later regret.

23   You need to increase your educational qualifications at this stage. This may not mean tertiary education, but learning new skills in your workplace will be essential.

24   Opportunities in the workplace arise suddenly, giving you the chance to climb the ladder of success faster than you previously imagined.

25   You have become too familiar with some of your friends and are starting to doubt their friendship. You might think that substitution is a splendid alternative. However, take a rethink on this.

26   Today, you may meet a poetic, and also quite discriminating individual. This chance encounter may impact on you and result in a new friendship.

27   Suspicious smiles in a medial gathering cause you to keep your distance. You may need to play along just to keep the peace.

28   You may have been finding it difficult to link some behaviours or dietary habits to the diagnosis of a physical problem. Now you might finally be able to connect the dots.

29 Be objective when making a decision about what you want professionally. Your judgement is sound at present.

30 Rather than pushing ahead too aggressively today, you are better off being more receptive and open-minded. Listen to the advice offered.

31 Try to avoid drinking to excess or, for that matter, doing anything without moderation in mind. You might suffer the consequences otherwise.

⊛ APRIL ⊛

Monthly Highlight

Your mind is on money this month, but you're rather emotional about it due to the placement of the Moon in your finance zone. Retrograde Mercury throws a spanner in the works too, over some educational or legal matter.

Venus entering your twelfth zone of secrets indicates that some family skeletons may come out, or that you have to withhold information from the ones you love. This could cause a stir.

---

1 Your energy levels are much lower than normal, so be careful not to make yourself susceptible to colds, the flu and other afflictions. Take your vitamins.

---

2 Perseverance is your key word today as you grind through your daily run-of-the-mill chores. There could be some frustration or confusion in fulfilling your obligations.

---

3 You may meet someone who can benefit your career just now. Socialise with those who can open doors.

4 You may accept an invitation to a film, theatrical event or some other entertainment, only to find you're disappointed by the result. It is best to keep your opinions to yourself.

5 You could be distracted by social activities that interfere with your work or other responsibilities. This can complicate the situation.

6 The full Moon is powerful just now, and shines a light on your inner self. Issues of contentedness, and how you can find happiness within yourself, will be your key focus.

7 You will be annoyed by others, especially if they are sleeping or slacking off around the home. You have a higher degree of sensitivity than usual, and will want to achieve much more than others can support you with.

8 There is no point contributing something if a negative state of mind is involved. Someone who agrees to help you is emotionally uncommitted. Don't accept this sort of assistance.

9 You are stimulated to express your creativity through some sort of culinary or cooking exercise. This can give you a great sense of satisfaction, and stimulate your tastebuds at the same time.

10 Resources can be scarce on the work front, so you will need to improvise. Be the master of inventing a solution out of nothing.

11 Dealing with government departments can be rather time consuming and frustrating. If you have an assistant, you need to delegate this sort of chore to them, so that your time is not eroded.

12 Looking forward to better times in your relationships requires letting go of the past. You may have an incident stuck in your gullet—you need to either swallow it or spit it out.

13 If you need to plea for someone to change, be succinct. Don't say too much, and get straight to the point.

14 You need to trace some lost information today. Along the line, some valuable piece of information has been misplaced. Correct your methods of filing.

15 For singles, a strong emotional or even sexual relationship could begin to develop today. However, it may be too heavy and quick for you to handle. Draw a line in the sand if that is the case.

16 Get organised, but don't get trapped in the details of what you are doing. It might be hard to do this today, especially if you are recovering from a night of fun!

17 Earth changes, along with climate and environmental issues might captivate your attention just now. Study these, but don't get caught up in fanaticism.

18 If you are inconsistent in the way you present information, you could be convicted on unfair grounds by your peers. Make sure you understand not just how to tell the truth, but how to get others to perceive you are doing so.

19 On the path of life you need to be a versatile pedestrian, so to speak, especially in work-related matters. Someone's outrageous behaviour may cause you to react, but tread lightly.

20 A promise of bigger and better things may seem lucrative, but could actually be invalid at this point in time. Investigate the fine print.

21 The new Moon indicates opportunities to move forward, but not in the way you think. Consider that rainy day, and put aside some money for it.

22 You can score big by attending a convention and giving your cause a good plug. Join forces with friends, because this has a social component to it as well.

23 You might oscillate between passion and cold aloofness today. You may not understand the intent of another, and could be caught off guard. As always, use intuition.

24 While you might be settled in the place you live, the place you work, or the way you are living your life generally, you also need to be sensitive to what changes are necessary. Start small, then involve the bigger things.

25 If someone is friendly but incompetent, it may actually cause damage to you. Again, you need to walk the tightrope delicately, finding the right balance between friendship and adequate distance.

26 Suppressed feelings need to come to the surface. Hiding yourself away from others—even if they are bothering you—won't solve the problem. Get out and talk about it.

27 Today, you should present yourself as unique by voluntarily expressing your logic. This will help someone in a problem and win you important Brownie points.

28 Don't waste your time on community or social activities that have no intended purpose other than chit-chat and idle gossip. You need to place greater value on your time just now.

29 Issues of licences and papers necessary to conduct yourself in business—or financially—will have you tearing your hair out. You need to be more adequately prepared.

30 If you are climbing the heights of financial fancy today, you need to be brought back to Earth. Dreams can only be fulfilled with practical, consistent work, and a good business plan.

Monthly Highlight

Connections with people from the past are double-edged swords. On the one hand, you may feel happy about bumping into them, yet on the other, you could feel as if your life hasn't developed in the same way as theirs. You mustn't play the comparison game.

Mercury and Uranus highlight your intellectual brilliance and capacity to get a lot of work done this month. Avoid impatience, though.

1   Today, you need to be wary of parrots who simply repeat what they have learned and try to ram their opinions down your throat. You will clearly see the pretenders.

2   You may have a problem with your mobile phone or some other communication device today. Over and above this, the way you communicate your ideas may be misunderstood. Clarity is your key word.

3   Putting together a brief autobiography can help you understand your past, and give you a greater capacity to predetermine your future. Jot down your life story.

4   You won't be delighted if your reputation is overlooked. This can even relate to taking the time to do someone in your family a favour and being dismissed. Try selfless service for its own sake.

5   Your moods could be unpredictable today, and what is an innocent expression on your part could be taken too seriously by others.

6   Don't be vague about investments. Your money may be spent unwisely just now. Get-rich-quick schemes won't work.

7   You might be shifting your perspective and, although doing so might be a little wearisome, you are making progress in understanding yourself and others. Why not try to inject a little fun into your philosophical explorations?

8   If you are in a company and working with other people, you sense the rules of engagement are changing. The company itself may be going down, in which case, it could be time to leave, even if that's a scary prospect.

9   Someone around you is paranoid today, probably because of your good work. They see you as an inconvenience, but being too nice to them will simply foster more of the same behaviour.

10   Today, you will have to clone yourself to get more work done, but regardless it won't be possible if you keep doing things the same way. Look at your work differently, and emulate those you respect.

11   You may experience a nervous episode with someone you love. Misinterpreting their actions could have you projecting your fears and making mountains out of molehills.

12   You mustn't give *carte blanche* to someone working on your behalf. Remember to sign off on transactions before they are cleared, especially if your money is involved.

13   You may well be fascinated by some newly introduced theological views, but don't let them shift your opinions, which are based on your personal experiences.

14   Associating with those who are more enlightened than yourself is a good way to lift your game and understand things beyond your current perception.

15 A package holiday is not a bad idea, especially if you don't have time to arrange all the details. Look at what's available, and you may just get a great price.

16 Don't be afraid to be straightforward in showing off your academic achievements today, if you have them. They will give you a considerable professional advantage.

17 In your current scenario you see a defect, and it's compulsory for you to speak up, even if you are a little apprehensive. This may impact on your employer.

18 You could be moderately idealistic, but your fear of speaking out may still be conspicuous. Measure each and every word before communicating today, especially if it's going to tarnish someone else's reputation.

19 You will be feeling a little drained by having to mirror someone else's behaviour. Stop chasing the truth on their behalf. Slow your pace, and simply enjoy good company.

20 This month's new Moon in your zone of friendships indicates that you need a mental breath of fresh air. Your peer group may have lost the art of democracy, and you want to extend your social circle.

21 If you are not sleeping well at the moment, midnight could be the most loathsome part of your day. Look into alternative methods of relaxation and sleep. Investigate healthy herbs.

22 You have to step away from the crossfire today, especially if someone has been blamed for some sort of sabotage. Remain neutral.

23 Complicating things can lead to contrary results, thereby causing disappointment. Don't expect too much from someone else today, because they may not deliver.

24 Your contempt for someone or something may well be meaningful, but will be matched in equal measure. Be careful, as you may hear some truths about yourself that aren't too complimentary.

25 You may be chosen just now to be the central figure in an initiative. Of course, it will take time, effort, and maybe even money. Are you up to the task?

26 You may be borderline on your spending versus your income. You need to embed some new guidelines so you can better manage your finances.

27 You may be irritated by a lawyer or some other government official who doesn't understand your situation. Explain yourself as best as possible, and leave it at that.

28 Today could find you attending a consultation or meeting in which you will need to be up to date on current trends and other affairs, otherwise you may feel uncomfortable.

29 You might go out somewhere, only to find the atmosphere worse than the one from which you were trying to escape. Remember that accepting invitations is not obligatory.

30 You will be upset today, but sometimes the greatest lesson is 20-20 hindsight. Putting out fires now is the result of a previous impulsive action on your part.

31 Interactive entertainment might be preferable to going out and mixing with others. Link up your television with the Internet or a media device, and enjoy having fun with the family.

⊚ JUNE ⊚

Monthly Highlight

Break free of your past, improve yourself, and see things in a completely new light. You have four planets activating one of the most spiritual zones of your horoscope this month. There could be an overload if you're not able to make head or tail of what's happening in your inner world. Talk to someone with experience. Mars challenges you, and your communications could be at odds with others. It's probably not a good time to sign a contract.

1 You could be tired of living in the property you are in, but consider this: have you been careless in making this home fit for your enjoyment and liveability? Reconsider what you have, and put some love and energy into your place of residence.

2 The suppressed devil in you emerges around this time, particularly if you are dealing with people less experienced than yourself. Shouting, however, is a waste of time. As always, lead by example.

3 Partitioning, setting limits and establishing order are part of a welcome division within the family unit. Everyone needs to know where they stand.

4 A full Moon is occurring in your zone of work and hygiene. You are suffering only because you failed to register some important information that was recently received. It's not too late to implement it now to regain your health.

5 You are missing out on many of life's free pleasures by attaching yourself too much to the television. Give it up for at least a few nights a week and rediscover other, more rewarding activities.

6 Your lover or partner has been unconscious in their actions, and you need to cushion the impact of the truth. Tell them how you feel, but do it in a polite way.

7 If you are dealing with a client or are in sales, you may be questioned on the infrastructure or cost-worthiness of your company. Be prepared to justify your position.

8 You could be angry from trying to research information on the Internet but being incapacitated by not having full bandwidth. Upgrade your telecommunication and Internet services.

9 You need to be stricter in dishing out privileges to those working underneath you. They will take advantage of you if you are not firmer.

10 You may be baffled by meaningless talk today, even though it doesn't seem meaningless to the one doing the talking. The question is, how much time can you spend dealing with people who are spouting nonsense?

11 You may feel insecure, especially while dwelling in archaic parts of your mind. Freshen up, cut the ties of the past, and move forward.

12 It is possible to change the cap—or the hat—of belief you are wearing, but only by studying comparative religions or philosophies adequately. You mustn't change on a whim.

13 Create a situation in which you can get work done uninterrupted and at length. Patchy or ad hoc routines will undermine your efforts.

14 The number 5 comes to me, telling me that this could be significant in some transaction or business dealing around this time. Keep it in the back of your mind today.

15 Don't loan money to a co-worker. If you have a secretary, he or she may take advantage of you today. Don't let their vulnerabilities victimise you.

16 You need to weather the storms of friendship—fluctuations in your emotions are part and parcel of life. Don't place too much stock in some of the changes that are occurring around you at the moment.

17 You may do something to serve or help another person, only to find them striking back for no apparent reason. Understand that they are reacting to another issue in their life and not to you.

18 You could feel that you are living in a parallel universe where no one seems to understand where you are coming from. Absence is often a great leveller and can win back respect.

19 You may feel slow, cosy and withdrawn, but also tense for no known reason. This is actually a significant message to you from within, and will require deep and diligent introversion.

20 What you are looking for is in your own library at home. You needn't go anywhere else to seek out information on, or an answer to, a particular question.

21 It's time for advertisements, magazines and other written forms of publicity. Be careful that everything is clear before committing to a payment.

22 You have to entertain people in high society as part of a work function today. You will feel the evening is tediously long. Sounds like a boring event.

23 Your spendthrift side will have you parting with a considerable amount of money around this time. There is no need to buy fancy items to express tasteful home decor.

24 You could be outraged at what you perceive to be unfair bank fees or other financial charges. Make your displeasure known.

25 You might be unconscious of the ramifications of words you are sharing with others. Be careful, otherwise someone may misrepresent you.

26 You may have promised someone a fee only to find that a third party you are negotiating with has different price tag. Be a master negotiator.

26 You mustn't send messages that don't have official approval today. Check with your superiors before appointing yourself the public relations and marketing manager.

27 There maybe some part of your home that appears ghastly to you. You need to take the time to transform it, but use the assistance of other members of the family. Solicit their help.

28 Your feelings are intense and, even though they are authentic, may scare someone off just now. Don't let your moods act to separate, but rather, to unite.

29 You must use methods of deterrence to stop lies. If you sense that someone is not being truthful, let them know before the words have a chance to emerge from their mouth.

30 A productive lifestyle also requires an expression of creative energies. Try to develop this by looking beyond your usual activities.

☉ JULY ☉

 Monthly Highlight

You might think something is wrong in your workplace and you could be worried about non-specifics. The Moon and North Node are notorious for this and will affect your work. Someone is pressuring you. You'll be giving a lot of your time for very little in return.

Mars indicates an industrious period, however, with physical work on your house and environment taking precedence, at least for a while. A growing frustration, due to the presence of Mars and Saturn, is evident, and you'll need to find an adequate outlet for your physical drives.

1 Expanding you education through a burst of digital wisdom is what is needed for your work practices just now. A clever and imaginative approach to your workload will give you kudos when others come to inspect what you've done.

2   You have to change your outlook due to an incident that has caused jealousy. Green eyes are all around you because you may be doing work of a higher standard than your co-workers.

3   It's a full Moon today. You may be emotional, and therefore your concentration will be slipping. Try to pay closer attention to the details of your work rather than clock-watching.

4   You need to consult a qualified medical practitioner. You mustn't waste time or money on alternatives if they haven't been tried and tested and referred to you by people who have used these services before.

5   If you can't find clothes that fit, especially if you're attending a special event, have you considered hiring a professional tailor instead? You might get something well made and reflective of who you are.

6   You're bothered by visuals just now, but may not be in a position to change what is, in the view of others, aesthetically pleasing. You'll simply need to put up with what you have.

7 You should pay attention to history so you don't make the same mistakes. You may be confused about how to deal with someone, but if you look back into the not-so-distant past, you'll quickly find your answer.

8 A brief explosion on your part is probably necessary today. Whoever is on the receiving end deserves every word that comes out of your mouth. Make no apologies for wanting to correct bad behaviour.

9 Although someone is a great organiser and a respected peer, you'll have to interrupt them if your viewpoint is better than theirs. They'll appreciate your input.

10 You need to improve your workspace to continually produce better work. If some of the furnishings, stationery supply holders or whatever are a little out of date, it's time to upgrade them.

11 If you're standing behind the customary way of doing things, you simply won't progress. The Moon is in the company of Uranus at the moment, which indicates the possibility of forging ahead with something bold and brilliant.

12 You need to wear the guise of a servant or otherwise humble person before considering gain today. If you come out with your guns blazing, you may ruin an opportunity to get ahead.

13 It may be time to move to a better town, or a least a place where people are like-minded and in sympathy with your views. You could feel as if even your best friends don't understand you at the moment.

14 You could be terrified—having a preview of what's to come in life—by coming across someone a little older who hasn't made the right decisions. Fortunately, you can correct your actions to avoid this outcome.

15 You need to discourage action well before it happens by sending some sort of notification to the culprit. On the other hand, being forewarned is forearmed.

16 You need to be negotiable on a mistake that you have made just now. It is obviously not something intentional, but by humbling yourself, you'll get back in the good books.

17 You mustn't be reluctant about fame, standing in the limelight and receiving some adulation today. People love to shower others with gifts, pat them on the back and feel good about doing so. Afford them that opportunity.

18 A direct mass-marketing campaign may not be the only way to get your point across, but now is a time when you should network yourself and, if need be, diagrammatically support what you're saying.

19 In the days of old, being portable wasn't part of our daily routine, but nowadays you need to get *mini*. Scale down. Look at how you can create more space by introducing some small and savvy electronics.

20 Butter wouldn't melt in the mouth of the queen bee right now, whoever she may be, but you can see through any posturing. You may need to make yourself a bigger queen than she is to level the score.

21 'Designer cosmology' means adapting beliefs to your needs, and making them practical. For example, today you might see a tie-in between money and your philosophical ideals.

22 If you're interested in someone, particularly a potential partner, you'll need to transmit your presence to gain their recognition. Once they know you're around, you can take the friendship to the next level.

23 Sidestepping mistakes requires you not only to see but to listen, and not just listen with your ears, but also your heart. Superficiality is discouraged in your reading—you need to look more deeply into things.

24 Be a grown-up pupil, and by that I mean listen intently to what others have to say, particularly if it's constructive criticism.

25 If admiration is what you're after during this cycle, the law of the universe is that you must first heap it on others. Try this, even though it seems to be back to front.

26 You might feel unsupported in your workplace today, particularly if you have an excess of e-mails, and your company is lacking a rescue plan for you. You need to work smarter, not necessarily harder.

27 You will be changing your dietary regime or cooking habits due to niggling family preferences at the moment. If they don't like what's on the menu, let them cook their own meals for a while.

28 You need to exhibit fiscal talent if you're going to carry your next bout of expenses. You may be on a shoestring budget but have the desire for some nice things, too. Creativity is necessary.

29 Pets could feature this week. If there's an animal you love that isn't well, you need to look into it.

30 Decrease the number of folk around you. Intermittently, you'll see me mentioning this, and today is no exception. Take a breather, collect your energies and reappraise your connections with others.

31 You have a bee in your bonnet at the moment and may want change, but will be obstructed in executing it. Stop pushing things around and let them open naturally, like a rose in bloom.

⊚ AUGUST ⊚

Monthly Highlight

Problems occur financially for a sibling or friend, and the way you handle this news is important. Meanwhile, Mercury and the Sun highlight your own finances, and there could be a conflict of interest between these two areas. A secret affair is indicated by Venus in the twelfth zone of hidden activities, meaning you might have a crush on someone and can't express it.

1   You will feel a temporary release of energy, a relaxation just now, after some sort of fight or confrontation. Release this intensity and enjoy the metaphorical breath of fresh air.

2   An attempt at democracy may fail and burn you today. You'll be reminded that, while we may live in a democratic society, our peer, family and work groups don't always operate the same way.

3   You could be excited after hearing an anecdote that inspires you to action, think differently and view life in a completely new light. Build on this.

4 You feel beautiful and glowing during this transit, and this has to do with what's happening within you, not necessarily without you. Cultivate inner attention and awareness.

5 A decision can come about only after consultation and agreement today. You have to fuse your mind with another person's, then allow the positive output to steer you both.

6 Unlock your potential creativity with a holiday, even if just for a few days. Make contact with someone you trust, and offer them the opportunity to share this experience with you.

7 Interactive web-logs, otherwise called blogs, are a part of modern information exchange. At first you may not understand how blogging can help you work, but you'll soon spot the possibilities.

8 Love may be in contraction as your vision of work eclipses your personal life. You may need to make some concessions, even though your loyalties are divided.

9 Causing a certain reaction in a friendship may be the only way get the ball rolling today. Although you have the support of most of your friends, one is being stubborn enough to hold things up.

10 The prevailing plan with friends may be split down the middle today, due to a sudden, uncompromising change of heart by someone. Be flexible in adapting.

11 You need to fiddle with business alternatives to become a master of money. Just now, your expenses reflect your desire to use things only as a means of satisfying yourself.

12 Be conservative at the start of a plan, because an idea you are promoting may be doomed due to its lacking a formula. Consultation is the key word for you today.

13 Your success will require some minor digging to access essential information. When you finally get it, you'll realise it's startling—but nevertheless essential—to get things on track.

14 You mustn't be impressed by clever jargon. This is a cunning ploy to reel you in, so be cautious when dealing with others today.

15 You may be shocked at some degrading atrocities you see in the news, and this will spur you towards making a financial donation. Even a one-off contribution can make a difference.

16 The only way you're going to get others to change their moral behaviour is to be the model of the very thing you want them to be.

17 Devilish cheats are often the hardest ones to pick, particularly in department stores. Count your change, check your receipts and don't for a minute think that a young, smiling face won't rip you off.

18 Secure your money and your belongings. Trust no one, and keep your eye on your bag in public places. This transit can indicate loss and even theft.

19 If there's a negotiation going down, you'll be irritated by the general consensus. Their arguments will have you bursting at the seams. Speak your mind.

20 Cheap satisfaction is at least a satisfaction of sorts. You needn't spend big to enjoy yourself and make it a memorable occasion.

21 Dust off those old photographs and memorabilia in the attic or basement, because the past has some appeal to you today. You'll have fun—albeit quietly and by yourself—rummaging through these old memories.

22 The ideological foundation of your family life may be at loggerheads with practical reality. When managing the family unit, don't be scared to try new things.

23 In your discussions today, be realistic and straight to the point. A significant breakthrough can be made with someone.

24 You'll discover the link between some of the things you possess and the expenses you are incurring. 'A grand waste' could be your final conclusion.

25 An appraisal of the quality of your skin is necessary, because this can reflect other changes within your body. Pamper yourself with a facial, massage, spa or other health remedies that will make you feel good.

26 A child is on the loose and you will need an upgraded scheme to get them back in line. You may feel you're temporarily making an enemy of one of your children, but it's necessary to regain order in the household.

27 No matter how well reasoned you are in the guessing game, you'll never get to the truth unless you ask the question. Perhaps you don't want to hear the truth?

28 Your supposed superiority may injure your reputation right now. Don't pretend to be more than you are. The secret is to be yourself.

29 You need to play the game of reverse assault if someone attacks your credibility. They won't see it coming, and you will get the upper hand by the end of the day.

30 Relax if you're under inquiry. If you've done nothing wrong in the past, everything will come out alright, and you'll be seen to be above reproach.

31 You'll be delighted at a reunion after a close struggle with someone. Minor issues were blown out of proportion. It's good to be friends again.

☉ SEPTEMBER ☉

 Monthly Highlight

Mars brings with it a sense of wonderful physical elation, competitiveness and physical vitality. Sports, outdoor activities and speculation will all be high on your agenda. However, if you have children, or deal with younger people, there may be problems associated with them. Try to step outside your normal viewpoint to gain a greater understanding of their perspective. Venus makes you attractive to potential partners.

1   Numerical classifications could bog you down. You need to check your calculations, but you may be doing so in a way that is giving you the same incorrect result. Stop, and reassess the problem.

2   Your craving for sweets is so strong that you could be hearing the chocolate calling your name. Your moods may also be subject to hormonal fluctuations.

3 An emergency situation at work demands you take command today. You may not have permission, but it is your duty to do so.

4 There is nothing worse than crossing the path of a prejudiced individual. Unfortunately, there may be nothing you can say or do about this person's attitude.

5 Someone you know may be rather eccentric in the way they direct things, but they shouldn't be judged. You must look at the motivation, not necessarily the action. This could be profitable to you.

6 Having insignificant flaws doesn't mean you are imperfect. You are comparing yourself to others and this makes you feel less than desirable. It's the whole package that counts.

7 Even trivial words have power, so don't underestimate your ability to persuade others today. Your friends will be feeling your impact.

8 A presentation, a suggestion you make, or simply some helpful advice could be viewed as impossible. You can only do your best; speak from your heart and let others take it or leave it.

9 Don't be too careless in firing or dismissing someone. You may not have all the facts surrounding the situation, and could be impulsive, especially if you're relying on second-hand information.

10 You'll be humoured and, at the same time, a little bit annoyed by a lousy postcard or message. Always remember, however, that it's the thought that counts.

11 You're concealing your hunger for affection. Today's a good day to express your needs, not hide them.

12 You may be inclined to spend more time in the office if your romantic situation is not in keeping with your ideals. This may give you some momentary breathing space, but don't make it a habit—hiding away might only make things worse.

13 Scratch around your memory and you'll see the correlation between what was done, what is happening, and what the likely outcome is.

14 Don't let literature upset you. A news item you read may get under your skin and upset your balance for the rest of the day. Be dispassionate in your assessment of things.

15 If you accidentally infringe on someone, promptly correct your mistake. That's enough to get the relationship back on track.

16 The new Moon is powerful now, and it gives you the ability to take verbal control over people who are trying to con you. Letting them know you understand their mind games will give you a feeling of great satisfaction.

17 An incoherent individual is not deserving of your time or help. Don't be duped by sweet words.

18 You may be tempted to purchase an 'abysmal ticket', that is, one that will give you a poor view, terrible sound and an overall bad experience. Don't waste your money.

19 A crazy dare by a friend may help you successfully secure a new friendship or, better still, a romantic affiliation. Here's your opportunity to take love to the next level.

20 You may be experiencing some anguish today due to your geographical location. If you're travelling great distances for your job, you have had enough. Seek an alternative.

21 You may be alarmed at a new policy being implemented either in your work, building or neighbourhood. There's no point whining: do something about it.

22 You need to wear unique loose-fitting garments today, because tight clothing may be affecting your moods and even your physical wellbeing. Rethink your wardrobe.

23 Don't be afraid to seek out an alternative form of entertainment tonight if your partner or lover is not in the mood. Moping around the house and begrudging them is not going to make you feel any better.

24 You need to look for hypothetical pathways to love. If you've crammed your brain full of preconceived ideas of an idyllic life and who your perfect partner is, you may be missing opportunities in the meantime.

25 You have a sneaking suspicion that something has recently been edited, concealed or removed from your view. Detective-like work is necessary for you to ferret out the truth.

26 Your love is, at best, slippery right now. If you've been inattentive to the needs of your partner, or they to yours, the relationship will need a reappraisal to put it back on track. Don't be lazy.

27 You may have a quarrel with an elderly person, possibly a family member or relative, over money. If this doesn't relate directly to you, it's better to sidestep the issue for the time being.

28 The opportunity to explore an unknown place will prompt you to frequent it much more. You may visit somewhere that seems to resonate with your inner self.

29 Professionally manipulating a situation could be fatal to your wellbeing. Be transparent and consultative if you have any problems.

30 The full Moon means you'll need the early detection of any symptom to work out proper solutions. You've previously turned a blind eye to the minor details of something much larger.

◎ OCTOBER ◎

 Monthly Highlight

You may be lucky financially, but only if you are careful with how you negotiate the fine print in a contract. You can play hardball, but you will need to do it in a diplomatic and gracious way. Don't let people take advantage of you.

The combined influence of the Sun, Mercury and Saturn highlight the importance of doing things slowly and diligently this month. If you can manage this, the powerful position of the Moon in Taurus will bring considerable benefits. The new Moon in your zone of home and family indicates a possible move and a new start.

---

1 You need to broadcast your thinking—loud and clear. Don't talk in riddles, because others won't get where you're coming from. Clarity in your communication equals success.

---

2 You should eagerly supply your help to someone, especially if they are significant to your overall strategy. Being useful to them ensures that karma will reciprocate.

---

3   Your appreciation of a friend should be measured because it could give them too big a head. Apart from that, they may feel that a copious amount of flattery is some sort of underhanded strategy to get something from them.

4   You must destroy any discrepancies that are seen in the eyes of others. Your reputation will be important now, and you must ensure that it is completely intact.

5   If you're looking at writing, expressing your thoughts and experiences on paper, you need to be motivated and disciplined on a day-by-day basis. Set aside even a small amount of time daily to chronicle your life.

6   You need to have a captive audience to establish your power base at the moment. You may be feeling lazy about what it takes to secure an alliance. Hard work will pay off.

7   You'll be feeling withdrawn today, but this gives you a chance to truly inhabit your purpose and believe in it totally. Convincing others means convincing yourself first.

8   A discussion may turn offensive and could lead to an acute accusation. This will be surprising and unwarranted. Be straightforward, and make sure you don't insult someone, even accidentally.

9   Remember that much of the spiritual material available to read is really just an overdose of intellectual information. Simply set your moral toggle to 'inner wisdom'.

10 Nip your raving compulsions in the bud, especially if you're haemorrhaging financially. This is an important cycle for taking full control over your money.

11 Greater efficiency will come through the expansion of your intellectual knowledge. Educational prospects are favoured now, so focus on becoming more skilled.

12 If you happen to be feeling unwell, please don't be a bad patient. There's nothing worse than people trying to extend their empathy only to have their hand bitten off.

13 Remembering a lost romance could trigger flights of your imagination. What's done is done, so don't continue to drag the past into the present or, worse still, into the future.

14 You could make new contacts virtually via websites and other electronic methods. Initially, you may be adverse to this, but the possibilities for making friends and lovers are endless.

15 It's a new Moon today, which means you'll need to make a daring bid for new beginnings. This has more to do with your emotional connection to others than anything else.

16 There may be an operational urgency at work. There could be malfunctions with computers or other electronic devices. You'll need to prepare yourself to solve the problem.

17 Financial leaks, especially of a speculative nature, will lead to a bank account imbalance. You need to check your statements, and not believe that the bank is always infallible.

18 You could be embarrassed being the star today, paraded in the limelight for being notably productive. But part of the game is to accept your accolades with grace and star-like quality.

19 Getting permission from someone who has no seniority is worthless. In fact, you might do something on the say-so of that person and cause yourself no end of problems. Seek out the right person in the first place.

20 Your overall vocabulary should be improved now, otherwise high-level communications may be misunderstood. Adopting new words can help you better express your feelings.

21 Before you commence work today, understand the prerequisites. The preamble is as important as the meat of the subject. Don't cut corners.

22 Today your relationships could be complicated, sailing on the ocean of feelings. The boat you're using to navigate uncharted waters needs to be fit for the storms ahead.

23 You want a contemporary assignment, not a Jurassic job. Boredom could set in, and it's time for you to look at what work alternatives are available.

24 You could feel like a child barred from an A-league game if you're introduced to a circle of snobs. Hold your head high, though. Don't pretend to be something you're not, and you'll win the respect of at least one person.

25 Even if your fashion is outdated you can still be magnetic. The greater part of attractiveness is your personality, not just your outfit.

26 You can link your state of mind to some addictive behavioural patterns right now. Try to be objective in weeding out any bad habits.

27 If you put the shoe on the other foot it will give you the chance to see things from another's viewpoint. However, you may not like doing it.

28 Don't ignore your bedroom as far as interior decoration is concerned. You spend so much time there, so it should reflect your inner space.

29 The full Moon means that you may be strapped for cash and could be for a little while longer. Believe it or not, you could save money by bringing your lunch from home and not spending so much on takeaway.

30 Unless you can overcome tunnel vision, you'll remain firmly tethered to your present life. This will deny you the pleasures you deserve. Break free.

31 It's the little things that cost you money. Have you ever added up what these incidental costs amount to over a month? Especially if you're a smoker. Over a year that expense could add up to a holiday.

◎ NOVEMBER ◎

Monthly Highlight

You may be separated from a friend this month, or a child if you are a parent. You must understand that the laws of nature indicate times for coming together and times for being apart. You mustn't see this as a negative thing. If you focus too much on the downside, it could be hard month for you.

Mercury and Mars prompt you to reassess your diet and exercise regimes this month. Workplace practices also need a rethink.

1 Although impressive opportunities seem to be coming your way, you're lacking in self-belief. The worst that can happen is that you'll get a no instead of a yes. Be prepared to try something new.

2 It's tempting to pass on that tidbit of gossip you've heard, isn't it? But think about how you'd feel if the tables were turned and the information was about you. Don't reveal secrets.

3 If you've been neglecting close friends due to work commitments, it's time to get out the address book and start reconnecting. It's a quiet day, but one that can be productive.

4 Be humble when you're presented an opportunity that could open doors for you. It could have gone to someone else, so be thankful that you've been considered for it.

5 Last-minute travel specials can save you considerable money, so it's important to make sure your passport is up to date and that you're ready to get out and enjoy yourself.

6 Walking may not be your preferred activity, but it will do your soul and body the world of good to get out on the beach or riverbank before sunset.

7 Spend a little time contemplating your financial strategy for the future today. You may realise you've overlooked something important, and that this now needs revising.

8 By checking your patterns of eating today, you'll come across the reason for your sluggishness and non-productivity. This also affects your finances and bank balance.

9   It may not be your style to hand out money to anyone who asks for it, but occasionally you come across a worthy cause. Be receptive, because you can make a difference.

10   It's time to build on your knowledge base and previous efforts to improve yourself. Expand your work or an interest that you've recently taken up.

11   Your generosity may have taken a bit of a beating lately, and you could be feeling overtaxed by giving and not getting. Your key word at the moment is selflessness.

12   Greater self-understanding lays in understanding your family roots, your genealogy and your personal history. Go back over the family history books to learn more about who you are.

13   Knowledge is power, and the new Moon indicates that spending time on a new subject will not be wasted. A work colleague may give you a hand with this. A relationship is now deepening.

14   An upgrade of plans made some time ago is overdue. You're avoiding this, but it's a good idea to update most things regularly to keep them on track.

15 Everyone likes to be liked, and you are no exception. However, someone at work may be baiting you, prodding you, even ignoring you. Try saying hello with sincerity.

16 At work, someone has knowledge that you can benefit from today. Don't be afraid to ask them to share it with you, because it can impact positively on the work you're currently doing.

17 You know the organising type of person in your social circle who goes ahead and books everything before asking anyone? They may be doing that right now, so quiz them.

18 Someone in your family, possibly even your partner, may be not doing as well as they are letting on. You need to be intuitive in seeking out their problem and helping them with it.

19 Work and friendships may overlap at the moment, but you need to be selective about how you do this. Often water and oil don't mix.

20 A friend in need can be a pain in the butt at times, but if it's a genuine problem, you must be a true friend to them, and help them as they have helped you in the past.

21 You could be disappointed by someone letting you down with a change of plans at the last minute. But, before you lose your head, let them explain things.

22 You could now start a new hobby or take up a course at an evening college for the sake of learning something new. A lecture could be inspiring.

23 Be firm and clear today when you air your grievances to someone who's been turning your world upside down. Sometimes others may not be aware of what they've done.

24 Your peer group at work is better informed on something than you are. Perhaps you missed a vital speech or presentation and you'll need to humble yourself and ask them to bring you up to speed.

25 You could decide to learn a foreign language or homemaking skill that could be the basis for meeting some like-minded people and making new friends.

26 You may meet someone new, but could feel some uncertainty about your feelings towards them. Rome wasn't built in a day, as they say, and neither was any long-term relationship.

27 Someone near you is out of their depth right now. Before diving in and saying yes to helping them, it's first a good idea to ask them what the nature of the problem is.

28 The full Moon today shows that you may be thinking about people who've moved away from your social circle, curious about where they are and what they're doing. Try using the Internet to find them again.

29 You could accidentally hear something about yourself that is not pleasant today, and you may not know how to deal with it. Remember, sticks and stones may break your bones but names will never hurt you.

30 Someone could let you down today, and this will hurt because you've supported them—and they've relied heavily on you—in the past. You need to let them know how you feel about this.

◎ DECEMBER ◎

 Monthly Highlight

You're passionate but argumentative this month, as Mars gains some power from its retrograde movement. Venus, in your zone of marriage, indicates reconciliation, but probably only after a tussle or two with the one you love. Kiss and make up.

The presence of Saturn in your area of creativity and speculation warns that you may need to slow things down, and that you could find it a little difficult coming up with new ideas. However, don't rush into anything.

1 You mustn't let fear dictate how you live. If you want to change—either your work or personal life—step out of the box, make the comparison, and then come to a conclusion.

2 Spending too much time socialising with workmates and friends could be eroding the time you spend on your work. Address this issue now to avoid immense pressure in the future.

3 Today, you can be grateful to others for their support of you. Limit your friendships and interactions only to those who deserve your love.

4 A pay rise or bonus is overdue and you may be mute on the subject, but you should be asking for what you feel you deserve. It only takes a phone call or, better still, a knock on the door of the boss's office.

5 Making your dreams a reality can sometimes seem a little expensive, but there's more than one way to get results. Look at how you can be most economical through sales, specials, and second-hand or used items.

6 Life just now might offer you a clue, or an account of a friend's beliefs and value systems. It's likely they're not the same as yours, but you can still learn from each other.

7 You need to turn a deaf ear to those who tell you you're mad, especially if it relates to spending money on your loved ones. It is, after all, your money.

8 Vital information, that may even be of value financially, should be guarded at all costs. Intellectual property or content that is private in nature should be held under lock and key for the time being.

9 Old problems may do a vanishing act, but unfortunately, they will always be replaced with new ones. You must simply take things in your stride.

10 Don't be tempted to dig into money you've set aside for bills today. Self-indulgence and a lack of discipline will only cause you hardship when the deadline for those bills arrives.

11 You need to spice things up in the bedroom just now, as your work commitments have become an unwelcome distraction. Set aside time for your lover.

12 Meditation may be necessary at present, especially if your stress levels are going through the roof. Put aside your work for half an hour, take the phone off the hook, and focus on yourself.

13 Stop swimming against the current—it's winning. Settle back, go with the flow, and do what is realistically possible. That's it.

14   You may imagine that someone in your workplace is undermining you, even if they've assured you otherwise. Stop projecting your insecurities onto those who are really there to help.

15   You have to support your partner or best friend because they have an opportunity that can change their lives. Don't question it, even if you are a little unsure about what they're doing. Just be there for them.

16   It's quite reasonable to be disappointed and even angry when someone close to you betrays your trust today, but you need to know the whole truth first. Sometimes there are facts beyond your perception.

17   Some of your ideas are a compilation of the input from others around you, so give credit where it is due and don't portray yourself as the sole originator. Today's key words are team spirit.

18   You have to correct someone who quotes you incorrectly. You need to be quick off the mark to do this so that further misunderstandings don't arise.

19 You have to postpone an event, outing or a journey today, due to a build-up of bills and expenses. It's not forever, though. You'll feel disappointed, but you know it's necessary.

20 A wolf in sheep's clothing will enter your social circle and could be difficult to stop. Look behind them to check their footprints.

21 If financial matters have been a niggling problem, it could be that you're earning less than you deserve. Sooner or later you're going to have to bite the bullet and ask for what you want.

22 There are givers and there are takers, actors and reactors. This is the ebb and flow of social and professional relationships. You firmly need to ask yourself which categories you belong to.

23 If you never move out of your tightly knit circle of friends and relatives, how can you expect to meet anyone new? It's time to be bold and adventurous by seeking out new people.

24 You want to achieve a lot just now, but can take on far too much. You're not going to be able to complete your tasks and satisfy everyone. This could result in broken promises on your part.

25 Credit card expenses could still be bothering you today. You may need to transfer the balance into a lower-interest repayment plan. Cut costs.

26 Buying expensive gifts for friends is not necessary. Bigger is not necessarily better. Sometimes the personal touch is what is needed.

27 Your living standards may not have changed significantly lately, and you're feeling frustrated that you can't lift yourself up to a higher echelon. Patience, my dear. Yet more hard work is needed.

28 The action of the Moon and Mars create a hair-trigger situation where you are likely to shoot from the hip. Think carefully before you speak. Words can't be taken back.

29 You are intense just now, and have your sights set on a goal, perhaps a personal one. But others could be irritated by your competitive attitude. Give them the chance to share their dreams as well.

30 Your finger is on the pulse at the moment, and you have a dynamic interest in other cultures, foreign lands and religions. Just for the heck of it you might try dining out at a restaurant that is completely different—Afghani, Mongolian, even African.

31 If you're planning to spend money on a holiday, make sure that there are some inclusions. You'd hate to see the bill after you've added food, Internet and other sundry items.

2012
ASTRONUMEROLOGY

A BREAK-UP IS LIKE A BROKEN
MIRROR. IT IS BETTER TO LEAVE IT
BROKEN THAN HURT YOURSELF TO
FIX IT.

Anonymous

THE POWER BEHIND
YOUR NAME

It's hard to believe that your name resonates with a numerical vibration, but it's true! Simply by adding together the numbers of your name, you can see which planet rules you and what effects your name will have on your life and destiny. According to the ancient Chaldean system of numerology, each number is assigned a planetary energy, and each alphabetical letter a number, as in the following list:

AIQJY	=	1	Sun
BKR	=	2	Moon
CGLS	=	3	Jupiter
DMT	=	4	Uranus
EHNX	=	5	Mercury
UVW	=	6	Venus
OZ	=	7	Neptune
FP	=	8	Saturn
—	=	9	Mars

Note: The number 9 is not allotted a letter because it was considered 'unknowable'.

Once the numbers have been added, you can establish which single planet rules your name and personal affairs. At this point the number 9 can be used for interpretation. Do you think it's unusual that many famous actors, writers and musicians modify their names? This is to attract luck and good fortune, which can be made easier by using the energies of a friendlier planet. Try experimenting with the table and see how new names affect you. It's so much fun, and you may even attract greater love, wealth and worldly success!

Look at the following example to work out the power of your name. A person named Andrew Brown would calculate his ruling planet by correlating each letter to a number in the table, like this:

A	N	D	R	E	W		B	R	O	W	N
1	5	4	2	5	6		2	2	7	6	5

And then add the numbers like this:

$$1 + 5 + 4 + 2 + 5 + 6 + 2 + 2 + 7 + 6 + 5 \quad = \quad 45$$

Then add $\quad\quad\quad\quad 4 + 5 \quad = \quad 9$

The ruling number of Andrew Brown's name is 9, which is governed by Mars (see how the 9 can now be used?). Now study the Name-Number Table to reveal the power of your name. The numbers 4 and 5 will play a secondary role in Andrew's character and destiny, so in his case you would also study the effects of Uranus (4) and Mercury (5).

Name Number	Ruling Planet	Name Characteristics
1	Sun	Attractive personality. Magnetic charm. Superman- or superwoman-like vitality and physical energy. Incredibly active and gregarious. Enjoys outdoor activities and sports. Has friends in powerful positions. Good government connections. Intelligent, spectacular, flashy and successful. A loyal number for love and relationships.
2	Moon	Feminine and soft, with an emotional temperament. Fluctuating moods but intuitive, possibly even has clairvoyant abilities. Ingenious nature. Expresses feelings kind-heartedly. Loves family, motherhood and home life. Night owl who probably needs more sleep. Success with the public and/or women generally.

Name Number	Ruling Planet	Name Characteristics
3	Jupiter	A sociable, optimistic number with a fortunate destiny. Attracts opportunities without too much effort. Great sense of timing. Religious or spiritual inclinations. Naturally drawn to investigating the meaning of life. Philosophical insight. Enjoys travel, explores the world and different cultures.
4	Uranus	Volatile character with many peculiar aspects. Likes to experiment and test novel experiences. Forward-thinking, with many extraordinary friends. Gets bored easily so needs plenty of inspiring activities. Pioneering, technological and creative. Wilful and obstinate at times. Unforeseen events in life may be positive or negative.

Name Number	Ruling Planet	Name Characteristics
5	Mercury	Sharp-witted and quick-thinking, with great powers of speech. Extremely active in life: always on the go and living on nervous energy. Has a youthful outlook and never grows old— looks younger than actual age. Has young friends and a humorous disposition. Loves reading and writing. Great communicator.
6	Venus	Delightful and charming personality. Graceful and eye-catching. Cherishes and nourishes friends. Very active social life. Musical or creative interests. Has great money-making opportunities as well as numerous love affairs. A career in the public eye is quite likely. Loves family, but often troubled over divided loyalties with friends.

Name Number	Ruling Planet	Name Characteristics
7	Neptune	Intuitive, spiritual and self-sacrificing nature. Easily duped by those who need help. Loves to dream of life's possibilities. Has healing powers. Dreams are revealing and prophetic. Loves the water and will have many journeys in life. Spiritual aspirations dominate worldly desires.
8	Saturn	Hard-working, ambitious person with slow yet certain achievements. Remarkable concentration and self-sacrifice for a chosen objective. Financially focused, but generous when a person's trust is gained. Proficient in his or her chosen field but a hard taskmaster. Demands perfection and needs to relax and enjoy life more.

Name Number	Ruling Planet	Name Characteristics
9	Mars	Extraordinary physical drive, desires and ambition. Sports and outdoor activities are major keys to health. Confrontational, but likes to work and play really hard. Protects and defends family, friends and territory. Has individual tastes in life, but is also self-absorbed. Needs to listen to others' advice to gain greater success.

YOUR PLANETARY
RULER

Astrology and numerology are intimately connected. Each planet rules over a number between 1 and 9. Both your name and your birth date are governed by planetary energies. As described earlier, here are the planets and their ruling numbers:

1 **Sun**

2 **Moon**

3 **Jupiter**

4 **Uranus**

5 **Mercury**

6 **Venus**

7 **Neptune**

8 **Saturn**

9 **Mars**

To find out which planet will control the coming year for you, simply add the numbers of your birth date and the year in question. An example follows.

If you were born on 14 November, add the numerals 1 and 4 (14, your day of birth) and 1 and 1 (11, your month of birth) to the year in question, in this case 2012 (current year), like this:

Add 1 + 4 + 1 + 1 + 2 + 0 + 1 + 2 = 12

1 + 2 = 3

Thus, the planet ruling your individual karma for 2012 would be Jupiter, because this planet rules the number 3.

YOUR PLANETARY
◎ FORECAST ◎

You can even take your ruling name number, as discussed previously, and add it to the year in question to throw more light on your coming personal affairs, like this:

A N D R E W B R O W N	=	9
Year coming	=	2012
Add 9 + 2 + 0 + 1 + 2	=	14
Add 1 + 4	=	5

Thus, this would be the ruling year number based on your name number. Therefore, you would study the influence of Mercury (5) using the Trends for Your Planetary Number table in 2012. Enjoy!

Trends for Your Planetary Number in 2012

Year Number	Ruling Planet	Results Throughout the Coming Year
1	Sun	**Overview**

The commencement of a new cycle: a year full of accomplishments, increased reputation and brand new plans and projects.

Many new responsibilities. Success and strong physical vitality. Health should improve and illnesses healed.

If you have ailments, now is the time to improve your physical wellbeing—recovery will be certain.

Love and pleasure

A lucky year for love. Creditable connections with children, family life is in focus. Music, art and creative expression will be fulfilling. New romantic opportunities.

Work

Minimal effort for maximum luck. Extra money and exciting opportunities professionally. Positive new changes result in promotion and pay rises.

Improving your luck

Luck is plentiful throughout the year, but especially in July and August. The 1st, 8th, 15th and 22nd hours of Sundays are lucky.

Lucky numbers are 1, 10, 19 and 28.

Year Number	Ruling Planet	Results Throughout the Coming Year
2	Moon	**Overview**

Overview

Reconnection with your emotions and past. Excellent for relationships with family members. Moodiness may become a problem. Sleeping patterns will be affected.

Love and pleasure

Home, family life and relationships are focused in 2012. Relationships improve through self-effort and greater communication. Residential changes, renovations and interior decoration bring satisfaction. Increased psychic sensitivity.

Work

Emotional in work. Home career, or hobby from a domestic base, will bring greater income opportunities. Females will be more prominent in your work.

Improving your luck

July will fulfil some of your dreams. Mondays will be lucky: the 1st, 8th, 15th and 22nd hours of them are the most fortunate. Pay special attention to the new and full Moons in 2012.

Lucky numbers include 2, 11, 20, 29 and 38.

Year Number	Ruling Planet	Results Throughout the Coming Year
3	Jupiter	**Overview**

Overview

A lucky year for you. Exciting opportunities arise to expand horizons. Good fortune financially. Travels and increased popularity. A happy year. Spiritual, humanitarian and self-sacrificial focus. Self-improvement is likely.

Love and pleasure

Speculative in love. May meet someone new to travel with, or travel with your friends and lovers. Gambling results in some wins and some losses. Current relationships will deepen in their closeness.

Work

Fortunate for new opportunities and success. Employers are more accommodating and open to your creative expression. Extra money. Promotions are quite possible.

Improving your luck

Remain realistic, get more sleep and don't expect too much from your efforts. Planning is necessary for better luck. The 1st, 8th, 15th and 24th hours of Thursdays are spiritually very lucky for you.

Lucky numbers this year are 3, 12, 21 and 30. March and December are lucky months. The year 2012 will bring some unexpected surprises.

Year Number	Ruling Planet	Results Throughout the Coming Year
4	Uranus	

Overview

Unexpected events, both pleasant and sometimes unpleasant, are likely. Difficult choices appear. Break free of your past and self-imposed limitations. An independent year in which a new path will be forged. Discipline is necessary. Structure your life appropriately, even if doing so is difficult.

Love and pleasure

Guard against dissatisfaction in relationships. Need freedom and experimentation. May meet someone out of the ordinary. Emotional and sexual explorations. Spirituality and community service enhanced. Many new friendships.

Work

Progress is made in work. Technology and other computer or Internet-related industries are fulfilling. Increased knowledge and work skills. New opportunities arise when they are least expected. Excessive work and tension. Learn to relax. Efficiency in time essential. Work with groups and utilise networks to enhance professional prospects.

Year Number	Ruling Planet	Results Throughout the Coming Year
		Improving your luck

Moderation is the key word. Be patient and do not rush things. Slow your pace this year, as being impulsive will only lead to errors and missed opportunities. Exercise greater patience in all matters. Steady investments are lucky.

The 1st, 8th, 15th and 20th hours of any Saturday will be very lucky in 2012.

Your lucky numbers are 4, 13, 22 and 31.

Year Number	Ruling Planet	Results Throughout the Coming Year
5	Mercury	**Overview**

Intellectual activities and communication increases. Imagination is powerful. Novel and exciting new concepts will bring success and personal satisfaction.

Goal-setting will be difficult. Acquire the correct information before making decisions. Develop concentration and stay away from distracting or negative people.

Love and pleasure

Give as much as you take in relationships. Changes in routine are necessary to keep your love life upbeat and progressive. Develop open-mindedness.

Avoid being critical of your partner. Keep your opinions to yourself. Artistic pursuits and self-improvement are factors in your relationships.

Work

Become a leader in your field in 2012. Contracts, new job offers and other agreements open up new pathways to success. Develop business skills.

Speed, efficiency and capability are your key words this year. Don't be impulsive in making any career changes. Travel is also on the agenda.

Year Number	Ruling Planet	Results Throughout the Coming Year

Improving your luck

Write ideas down, research topics more thoroughly, communicate enthusiasm through meetings—this will afford you much more luck. Stick to one idea.

The 1st, 8th, 15th and 20th hours of Wednesdays are luckiest, so schedule meetings and other important social engagements at these times.

Throughout 2012 your lucky numbers are 5, 14, 23 and 32.

Year Number	Ruling Planet	Results Throughout the Coming Year
6	Venus	**Overview**

Overview

A year of love. Expect romantic and sensual interludes, and new love affairs. Number 6 is also related to family life. Working with a loved one or family member is possible, with good results. Save money, cut costs. Share success.

Love and pleasure

The key word for 2012 is romance. Current relationships are deepened. New relationships will be formed and may have some karmic significance, especially if single. Spend time grooming and beautifying yourself: put your best foot forward. Engagement and even marriage is possible. Increased social responsibilities. Moderate excessive tendencies.

Work

Further interest in financial matters and future material security. Reduce costs and become frugal. Extra cash is likely. Additional income or bonuses are possible. Working from home may also be of interest. Social activities and work coincide.

| Year Ruling | Results Throughout the Coming |
Number Planet	Year
	Improving your luck
	Work and success depend on a creative and positive mental attitude. Eliminate bad habits and personal tendencies that are obstructive. Balance spiritual and financial needs.
	The 1st, 8th, 15th and 20th hours on Fridays are extremely lucky this year, and new opportunities can arise when they are least expected.
	The numbers 6, 15, 24 and 33 will generally increase your luck.

Year Number	Ruling Planet	Results Throughout the Coming Year
7	Neptune	**Overview**

Overview

An intuitive and spiritual year. Your life path becomes clear. Focus on your inner powers to gain a greater understanding and perspective of your true mission in life. Remove emotional baggage. Make peace with past lovers who have hurt or betrayed you. Forgiveness is the key word this year.

Love and pleasure

Spend time loving yourself, not just bending over backwards for others. Sacrifice to those who are worthy. Relationships should be reciprocal. Avoid deception, swindling or other forms of gossip. Affirm what you want in a relationship to your lover. Set high standards.

Work

Unselfish work is the key to success. Learn to say no to demanding employers or co-workers. Remove clutter to make space for bigger and better things. Healing and caring professions may feature strongly. Use your intuition to manoeuvre carefully into new professional directions.

Year Number	Ruling Planet	Results Throughout the Coming Year
		Improving your luck

Maintain cohesive lines of communication and stick to one path for best results. Pay attention to health and don't let stress affect a positive outlook. Sleep well, exercise and develop better eating habits to improve energy circulation.

The 1st, 8th, 15th and 20th hours of Wednesdays are luckiest, so schedule meetings and other important social engagements at these times.

Throughout 2012 your lucky numbers are 7, 16, 25 and 34.

Year Number	Ruling Planet	Results Throughout the Coming Year
8	Saturn	**Overview**

Overview

This is a practical year requiring effort, hard work and a certain amount of solitude for best results. Pay attention to structure, timelines and your diary. Don't try to help too many people, but rather, focus on yourself. This will be a year of discipline and self-analysis. However, income levels will eventually increase.

Love and pleasure

Balance personal affairs with work. Show affection to loved ones through practicality and responsibility.

Dedicate time to family, not just work. Schedule activities outdoors for increased wellbeing and emotional satisfaction.

Work

Money is on the increase this year, but continued focus is necessary. Hard work equals extra income. A cautious and resourceful year, but be generous where possible. Some new responsibilities will bring success. Balance income potential with creative satisfaction.

Year Number	Ruling Planet	Results Throughout the Coming Year

Improving your luck

Being overcautious and reluctant to attempt something new will cause delay and frustration if new opportunities are offered. Be kind to yourself and don't overwork or overdo exercise. Send out positive thought-waves to friends and loved ones. The karmic energy will return.

The 1st, 8th, 15th and 20th hours of Saturdays are the best times for you in 2012.

The numbers 1, 8, 17, 26 and 35 are lucky.

Year Number	Ruling Planet	Results Throughout the Coming Year
9	Mars	

Overview

The ending of one chapter of your life and the preparation for the beginning of a new cycle. A transition period when things may be in turmoil or a state of uncertainty. Remain calm. Do not be impulsive or irritable. Avoid arguments. Calm communication will help find solutions.

Love and pleasure

Tremendous energy and drive help you achieve goals this year. But don't be too pushy when forcing your ideas down other people's throats, so to speak. Diplomatic discussions, rather than arguments, should be used to achieve outcomes. Discuss changes before making decisions with partners and lovers in your life.

Work

A successful year with the expectation of bigger and better things next year. Driven by work objectives or ambition. Tendency to overdo and overwork. Pace your deadlines. Leadership role likely. Respect and honour from your peers and employers.

Year Number	Ruling Planet	Results Throughout the Coming Year
		Improving your luck
		Find adequate outlets for your high level of energy through meditation, self-reflection and prayer. Collect your energies and focus them on one point. Release tension to maintain health.
		The 1st, 8th, 15th and 20th hours of Tuesdays will be lucky for you throughout 2012.
		Your lucky numbers are 9, 18, 27 and 36.

The World of Mills & Boon®

There's a Mills & Boon® series that's perfect for you. We publish ten series and with new titles every month, you never have to wait long for your favourite to come along.

Blaze®

Scorching hot, sexy reads

By Request

Relive the romance with the best of the best

Cherish™

Romance to melt the heart every time

Desire™

Passionate and dramatic love stories

ENDTIME ECONOMICS

ECONOMICS

RECESSION OR POSSESSION

GW00601019

JOAN HUNTER

ENDTIME ECONOMICS:
Recession or Possession

Joan Hunter Ministries
PO Box 777, Pinehurst, Texas 77362-0777
www.joanhunter.org

ISBN: 978-0-9829516-0-6

Printed in the United States of America

Dedication & Acknowledgements

This book is dedicated to those who will read and implement what is in this book and be able to give more to God.

A thank you to the many people who added to this book and shared their incredible testimonies with me of how God came through when there was no way.

Special thanks to my daughter, Charity Bradshaw, for my great hair style and make up – not to mention a great picture on the About the Author page at the back of this book.

My husband, Kelley Murrell, who helped me with editing, Naida Johnson (RN, CWS, FCCWS) who helped pull it all together, and Beth Carley who made the corrections.

Nathanael White and David Sluka for their editorial work and management of this project. Steve Fryer for the cover design.

Introduction

As a young girl growing up in Florida, my mom, my brother, and I experienced some REALLY tough times.

My mom was a single mom and started a secretarial company to try to support us. Our treat was bologna once a week. That was the only meat we would get for the week except what we received in school.

I remember going behind a grocery store where my mom helped my brother crawl into a dumpster to retrieve a bushel of bad peaches. We went home and Mom cut up the whole bushel (trying to find parts that could be eaten) so my brother and I could have a small bowl of fruit. We did not know the Lord at that time.

I thank God for getting us through those tough times. Just as God turned total devastation and poverty into incredible blessings, He can do it for you, too!

I believe that as you read the pages of this book, God will open your eyes to ALL He has for you – so that you walk in prosperity greater than what you have ever experienced in your life.

Most people pay attention to the news these days whether from the TV, radio, Internet, or moment-by-moment updates on the Internet. I want to remind you that the news you hear from these sources is from man's perspective, not God's. Yes, you must be informed about world events. How else can you pray for change or rejoice when God's promises manifest in front of your eyes? There is always good news and bad news available even though too often most of the emphasis seems to be on the negative.

However, the "news" that endlessly bombards you 24/7 should not be your primary source of information – especially when it comes to your finances. Too often, we depend on the newscasters to tell us what is happening around the world. As a believer, to learn what will occur in your immediate world, you must turn instead to the Word of God. The more you depend on the Word, the greater your life will be.

"For I know the thoughts that I think toward you,"
says the LORD, "thoughts of peace and not of evil,
to give you a future and a hope."
(Jeremiah 29:11)

He does have your best interests in mind. He has only good things for you; however, you have to turn to Him and open your mind and heart to hear, understand and follow His plan for you.

Faith comes by hearing,
and hearing by the word of God.
(Romans 10:17)

When you turn to the Word of God, you receive Good News and learn what He has in store for you. Listening to the world's news as a constant diet produces nothing but fear, worry and anxiety. God gives you free choice. What will you choose? Which news do you want to hear?

Well, I have some great "news" for you! This new information can change the rest of your life, multiply your finances, and transform you into all that God created you to be.

Change the Way You Think

Many people have developed a mindset embedded in poverty or recession and fully expect to experience loss, depression and defeat. They are blind and deaf to any other information no matter how convincing the argument. They are living with the mindset of poverty. Many are trapped by the spirit of poverty and appear to be satisfied living below God's best.

***

You can get free from the spirit of poverty, but still have a mindset of poverty.

***

Since you are reading this book, you obviously are not satisfied living on "Just-Getting-By Street" and want to move up the ladder to success. Repeat this simple prayer:

"Father, I thank You for Your Word that says, You have given ME the power to get wealth. I break the spirit and mindset of poverty off of me and everything I do. I thank You for giving me a mind to use. I thank You for giving me the talent to do what You have given me to do. Father, I thank You for blessing my finances. Any hindering forces that are keeping me from receiving more, I command them to be gone. I want more to give more. And I thank You, Father, because You are my One and only true Source, in Jesus' Name. Amen."

Please understand that you can be set free from the *spirit* of poverty, but still have one foot trapped in the *mindset* of poverty. You can be a born again believer but still find yourself making decisions from the viewpoint of poverty if you do not understand how Christ thinks. Some people expect to be poor and experience loss regardless of the daily blessings God is giving to them.

The mind of Christ does not have any connection to the mindset of poverty or the mentality that traps you into poverty. The Kingdom of God is an ever-increasing Kingdom, not one in a state of decline or recession.

***

We are being transformed from

glory to glory, not from glory to gory!

***

Let me give you an example. One day some-one told me that they needed a new vehicle. I quickly said, "Then it is time to pray that God will give you a miracle vehicle." We prayed. They are now the blessed owners of a new vehi-cle: $10,000 less than retail, three years old, with only 30,000 miles, and fully loaded with leather seats and all the other extras.

***

We prayed, they believed,

God gave and they received.

***

A mindset or spirit of poverty will make you think that you are on your own, that you have no support when you have a need or face a "giant" in your life. Nothing could be further from the truth. You are never alone. God is al-ways there for you and with you. Jesus is always accessible to help with every situation.

The mind of Christ understands that God wants to bless you with wonderful blessings in all areas of your life. When you ask, God will give you more than you can ask, hope, or dream. Read the words of Jesus and the Apostle Paul:

"If you then, being evil, know how to give good gifts to your children, how much more will your heavenly Father give the Holy Spirit to those who ask Him!"
(Luke 11:13)

Now to Him who is able to do exceedingly abundantly above all that we ask or think, according to the power that works in us
(Ephesians 3:20)

When you have God's help, trusting in the news reports or your natural abilities is not the ultimate answer. God will do so much more for you than you could ever accomplish with your own wisdom or strength. God will go so far above and beyond your expectations to show you He is alive and well. He wants to bless you – not based on your education or what you can do for yourself, but based on your faithfulness to His Word.

I know a wonderful man of God from west Texas. One night God gave him a dream. The next morning, he drew an architectural design for a new piece of machinery. He took it to an engineering firm and said, "I want to show you something. What do you think about it?"

After looking over the design, the amazed engineers looked at him and said, "This is the most intricately designed piece of machinery we have ever seen. Where did you get your engineering degree? Where did you ever come up with this?" He replied, "I got it in a dream." One engineer asked, "You got it in a what?" He said, "I got it in a dream."

In the end, he made millions of dollars from a God-given design. He did not receive the dream because he was an engineer. He did not have an engineering degree. He did not even finish the ninth grade. God simply gave him the dream. He obediently wrote everything down, presented it to the right company and was blessed with millions of dollars. God confounded the wise with something seemingly foolish to man's understanding.

But God has chosen the foolish things
of the world to put to shame the wise,
and God has chosen the weak things of the world
to put to shame the things which are mighty.
(1 Corinthians 1:27)

Not only that, God did not stop there. Because this man was obedient, God gave him another dream. When God finds He can trust an obedient servant, He will continue to bless them with more!

God will do this and more for anyone who trusts Him. Does the Word of God say, "Trust in the *news* with all your heart, and *YOU* shall direct your path"? NO! His Word tells us what to do.

> *Trust in the LORD with all your heart,*
> *and lean not on your own understanding;*
> *in all your ways acknowledge Him,*
> *and He shall direct your paths."*
> (Proverbs 3:5)

How many people do you know who trust the news without question? They are totally consumed with and are "leaning" on the opinions of man as their ultimate source of knowledge. They frequently check the Internet for the latest events, listen to radio newscasts in the car, and watch TV news programs for hours every night and weekend. Then they wonder why they do not have peace and joy.

Frequently, a spirit of fear enters the mind along with the negative information from these seemingly innocent news reports. By believing and accepting the negative "junk" as truth and reality, a person also invites a spirit of fear into their lives.

*Faith comes by hearing
and hearing by the Word of God.*
(Romans 10:17)

Yes, we have often heard that faith comes by hearing the Word of God. What we sometimes forget is that fear comes by hearing what is around you – the news according to man. It is your choice to invite faith or fear into your life based on what you listen to and welcome into your spirit.

Choose what enters your mind very carefully. Use God-given discernment. Draw on the mind of Christ within you. Is what you hear about finances bringing peace to your soul? Or is it bringing anxiety and fear? Are your words spoken to others adding peace to them or causing unrest and pain? Learn, choose to make God choices in what you feed on, what you hear.

Embrace the Mindset of Prosperity

Another man I know was complaining about losing both his car and house. Even though he was a very influential leader, he spoke from a mindset of poverty.

Personally, I would never allow those words to come out of my mouth. Instead, I am planning to pay off my home and at the time of writing this book, I paid off my car. I am prepared to receive more and more and more, far above and beyond anything that I have ever received before.

I believe I will have more than enough. I "plan" to receive and I "plan" what I will do with His blessings when they arrive. My "expector" is up every day of my life.

***

I expect to receive.

This is the hour for Christians to be

more prosperous than ever before.

***

This is the hour for Christians to be more prosperous than ever before. You need to be a bright light to the world as you prosper supernaturally in this environment of doom and gloom that the world is choosing to experience.

Let others know your Source is God and you cheerfully expect to be blessed.

All four of my girls, my sons-in-law, and I have gotten new cars in the last few years. Two of the girls are extremely busy with their own businesses. The other two have gotten raises. One received a $15,000 a year increase in pay.

I believe their blessings have partially come from me because the blessings of God are on my life, as well as the blessings that have come down from my parents. Of course, my children are also faithfully following the principles I am sharing with you so they can receive His best for their lives.

***

He is taking you and me

from recession to possession!

***

These are just a few examples of how powerful a renewed mind can be. Think with the mind of Christ. The world will appear entirely different to you and you will make wiser decisions.

When we set our minds in agreement with the promises in the Word of God, we can expect incredible blessings from our Father. God is supernaturally blessing His people!

And you shall remember the LORD your God,
for it is He who gives you power to get wealth,
that He may establish His covenant which
He swore to your fathers, as it is this day.
(Deuteronomy 8:18)

Recently while studying this Scripture, God revealed a key within that one verse of Scripture. It is HE that gives YOU the power to get wealth. He is certainly able to just give you wealth; however, He goes beyond just a gift. HE gives you the ability and the wisdom on how and where to get wealth. Of course, God often blesses us with gifts or wealth, which we have not worked for; however, the majority of the time, WE have to allow God to use us to PRODUCE the increase in our finances.

And so God can always point to us as
examples of His incredible wealth of His favor
and kindness toward us, as shown in ALL He
has done for us through Christ Jesus.
(Ephesians 2:7)

Live by Heaven's Reality

One woman explained to me that her husband cannot stay away from the news. He listens, watches, or reads the news all day long and late into the nighttime hours. Fear not only invades his mind daily but is now permeating their marriage and family. He happens to be in the news business and she is having problems dealing with him. He is consumed with words that draw fear into his life and their home.

Another woman told me about her children. None of them are following the Word of God. They have all lost their jobs and are battling all kinds of problems. Fear and poverty have overtaken their lives, their souls and their spirits. They are not walking in faith. They have not made good choices. They are following the world's advice.

We walk by faith, not by sight.
(2 Corinthians 5:7)

Jesus taught His disciples to pray, "On earth, as it is in heaven." There is no lack and no sickness in heaven and there should not be on this earth either.

Faith is the substance of things hoped for,
the evidence of things not seen.
(Hebrews 11:1)

When you choose to put your faith in the news, you lose your faith in God. Without His help, you live by your own strength as you react to what you see happening around you.

The reality is that some Christians are not losing jobs or receiving cutbacks. We are being blessed as we take our eyes off the world and stop depending on man. We are to turn to Him and believe in Him.

Not that I have already attained,
or am already perfected; but I press on,
that I may lay hold of that for which
Christ Jesus has also laid hold of me.
(Philippians 3:12)

Possess the Land God Has For You

"If my people who are called by My name
will humble themselves, and pray and seek
My face, and turn from their wicked ways,
then I will hear from heaven and will forgive
their sin and heal their land."
(2 Chronicles 7:14)

This is a powerful promise from God; however, it does come with a condition. First, you have to act, and then He will respond to your actions. As a believer, you are to forsake the world, join with other believers, and pray. By seeking His face and staying away from wicked ways, you are placing your trust in Him. When you do what He asks, He responds with unbelievable blessings.

The Bible says God will *"heal their land."* Corporately, believers often get together and pray for our country, but God showed me that *land* means so much more. Yes, God promised physical land to Abram, but the blessing God had in mind extended way beyond that small area of property.

> *Now the LORD had said to Abram:*
> *"Get out of your country, From your family*
> *And from your father's house,*
> *To a land that I will show you.*
> *I will make you a great nation;*
> *I will bless you*
> *And make your name great;*
> *And you shall be a blessing.*
> *I will bless those who bless you,*
> *And I will curse him who curses you;*

And in you all the families of the earth
shall be blessed."
(Genesis 12:1-3)

What is *your* land? I believe the "land" God has for you to possess includes your body, your home, your transportation, your job, your family – everything related to you and your life! Think of it on a very personal basis.

When you look at it that way, you have to make a personal choice to stay away from wicked ways. Your focus changes from your own reasoning and human wisdom on how you can fix your problems to the greatness of your good God and His ability to save you from any negative circumstance. When you choose to focus on Him, then God will speak His wisdom, His plans, His blessings and His prosperity into your life.

Pursue Prosperity in All Things

I faithfully pray over both the ministry's finances as well as my personal finances every day. I praise God that my every need is met on a regular basis. Kelley and I lay hands on our checkbooks (ministry and personal) and pray that there will always be enough, and more than enough. As I have believed the promises of God to bless us, the ministry finances have increased even in the midst of recession. Don't ever limit God.

> *Beloved, I pray that you may*
> *prosper in all things and be in health*
> *just as your soul prospers."*
> (3 John 2)

Prosperity does not only mean money. It includes life, love, health, and hope. Your heavenly Father wants you to walk in health in all areas of your life – physical, mental, spiritual as well as financial.

Stay humble. Stay away from evil. Stay in the Word. Stay free from sin. Feed your spirit. You will walk in more abundance than you have ever believed you would have in your lifetime.

In the middle of all the financial problems of 2008-2009, our ministry moved. Personally, my husband, Kelley, and I also relocated. Just the logistics alone of such an undertaking could have been overwhelming. Keep in mind, I continued to travel wherever God sent me during this period of time.

We know without a doubt that we heard God. All our needs have been met super-naturally. We have more space than ever before and it is an absolutely gorgeous area. We are so excited about His blessings and know there are more to come as we faithfully follow His leading.

Our prosperity is based on the Word of God, as our soul prospers. We feed ourselves on the things of God frequently and regularly, making our souls prosper. As our souls prosper, our bodies and minds prosper. The effects of our blessings overflow to every corner of our lives.

Is everything in our lives sweet peaches and cream 24/7? No, we still live on earth and are faced with challenges daily. However, we are so blessed that we just hop over the challenges to catch the next blessing. We listen to His Word, speak His Word and believe His Word.

When you spend hours on the Internet, reading newspapers, and listening to TV news anchors broadcasting their negative messages, what will enter your mind? What will come out of your mouth? Negativity. Junk. Trash. Fear. Poverty.

Cut Back on the Right Things

We have all heard that we need to "cut back" in every aspect of life in order to survive. Some people have even considered decreasing their giving into God's work. Perhaps they plan on going to church once a month instead of every week to save money on gas. Cutting back in these areas is not a wise choice. Instead, limit some expensive daily habits such as 3-4 cups of specialty coffee every week, going out to eat several times a week or watching TV numerous hours a day.

"Oh, no! I can't give up my coffee or my shows!" Some people are quite willing to cut back on spiritual things that can nourish the inner man, but insist on hanging onto personal things that only feed the body or soul on a temporary basis. Their priorities are upside down.

Personally, I cannot stop giving my tithes and offerings. I cannot stop giving to God and I do not want to stop or cut back. I will continue to follow His instructions regardless of what man says. He is my Source! He is my Father!

You cannot cut back on giving to God either. He wants to be first in your life and always knows what is best for you. His wisdom is always available if you ask for it. Choose His will as top priority in your life and everything else will fall in place, especially your finances.

Money is like seed. You use some of it to make bread to eat and some to sow into good ground to produce a harvest for the future. From that abundance, you can be generous and reach out to others with His Good News.

The apostle Paul explained this principle to the Corinthians so long ago. It still applies to us today.

Now may He who supplies seed to the sower, and bread for food, supply and multiply the seed you have sown and increase the fruits of your righteousness, while you are enriched in everything for all liberality, which causes thanksgiving through us to God.
(2 Corinthians 9:10-11)

What happens if you turn all your seed into bread by wasting it on expensive habits? You rob yourself of the prosperity God intends for you when you eat all your seed, leaving nothing to sow into your future. People are spoiled these days with all the newest toys and fashions. Expensive habits need to be trimmed. God-given seed needs to be planted regularly into the well of eternal wisdom and life.

This principle is so important to understand and put into practice. Your life literally depends on it. Do not eat your seed. Plant it so it can multiply into a bountiful harvest.

A professional financier recently explained that we need to understand scriptural endtime economics. Instead of "name it and claim it," we need to put some fire behind it.

When we get our finances lined up with the Word of God, our finances will be blessed – unbelievably, incredibly blessed – and we will move out of the recession into possession of what God has for planned for us.

Plant in Good Soil

So often people attend a special church service and out of habit toss some cash or a check into the offering. Whenever you give, wherever you give, you need to make certain it is being planted in good soil. Do some research. You would not send your child to a school with a reputation of producing undereducated graduates who could barely read. You want your child's time well spent in a school where they will learn what they need to know to be successful in college and on into the job market.

You also would not bring mediocre or bad food into your home to feed your family. Your loved ones would not grow. They would not thrive. Instead, they would grow ill and possibly die from poor nutrition. Buying or investing in less than the best is wasting your hard earned money.

Giving to God should follow the same principle. There are numerous people and ministries available and eager to receive your offerings. Researching their statement of faith or the work they are doing is not difficult when the Internet is so available. Find out about their missions giving. Ask about their goals and where they are headed. Use wisdom. Make sure your offerings will have the maximum effect possible for His kingdom.

If you discover there is nothing going on in that church or that ministry, you are planting your finances into dead ground. There will be a "crop failure" because your seed will not grow or prosper in that soil.

You would not take valuable seeds of grain or corn and throw at rocky soil where nothing can grow or thrive. A harvest would be impossible. The same principle applies to your tithes and offerings. Ask God where He would have you plant your seed. He knows where the best fertilized soil is located. He knows where the blessings will multiply into abundance.

We see hundreds of people healed every week. We minister to countless thousands every day. God is doing incredible things! New lungs, new female organs, surgeries cancelled by the doctors after getting healed.

A few years ago, a lady came up to me in Portersville, California. She had been diagnosed with Stage IV lung cancer and was not expected to live. I laid hands on her, cursed the cancer, and spoke a new set of lungs into her body.

She went back to her doctor two weeks later. The doctor took X-rays, examined them very closely and came to her with a look of bewilderment on his face. He said, "I don't know what you did, but you have two new lungs!!!" It was exciting to see her the following year totally healed. Praise God!

When you give your seed to a church or a ministry where miracles are happening, your finances and personal ministry will also experience a miracle. You will share in the anointing of that ministry or lack thereof. Give to a dead church, your seed will be buried and die. They take it and use it, however it doesn't accomplish anything or go anywhere. You have wasted your hard-earned money. You feel like they have "taken" your finances.

Many people give to charity. If you are thinking about or are in the habit of doing so, I simply caution you to pray about it. Make sure God tells you where to plant your gifts. Do your research. Sometimes your research will be to listen and give where, when and what God tells you to.

I do not "take" offerings; I "receive" offerings. God also "receives" your offerings. When He tells you to "give" offerings or alms to the poor, you can be sure He is tearing down the hindrances holding back your finances. He always supplies provision to complete what He plans. If He is telling you to plant something special, He has something special planned for you.

Your seed will be in preparation for a special harvest.

God is pouring out His blessing on us. As this book is being written, the ministry's land is covered with beautiful grass that is nourishing some cows. Soon that land will have buildings that will feed hungry people called by God to be trained and sent out to the 4 corners of the world to minister to the hungry and lost.

We have a great big vision. We do not want a little building in a strip mall to feed a few people at a time. We want facilities to minister, feed, and train hundreds at a time.

Sometimes we have to do things one step at a time, or one person at a time. Because things are moving faster these days and God's timetable is counting down, we need more and more people out ministering to the lost. We need our efforts and our offerings to be optimized. We believe in multiplication, not just addition.

More than one person has expressed the desire to invest large sums of money into developing our property into the international healing and conference center that we have envisioned. The desire is there, the willingness is there to actually pay for at least one of the buildings; however, the finances have been held up on their end. There is a huge hindrance holding things back.

Are you experiencing a similar blockade? Whatever is blocking your finances, you must pray positive words over your business no matter what your profession is. Declare positive things. Speak increase and prosperity. The words of your mouth will determine your success, not the words of worldly newscasters.

Give into the Kingdom

All the demons in hell and the devil himself are afraid of the millions of dollars God has planned for you. Because they know what you will do with the money, the devil and his minions want to block your prosperity!

One gentleman received $30 million dollars in settlements. This single man bought four cars and two large homes, and chose not to tithe off his settlement. The government took $18 million for income taxes. If he had tithed, his taxes would have been about $2 million. Think of what those millions could have done for the Kingdom. Not only that, but tithing would have thrown the door wide open for God to continue to bless him.

We need to give whenever God blesses us. Guess what? He blesses us every day, though not always monetarily. Whatever way He blesses you, immediately look for a way to give in kind.

For example, my daughter needed a car. She prayed with her husband about it. Because she was going back to school, their budget was dependent totally on his income. In order to cut back, she proposed, "We could cut back on our missions giving." He immediately replied, "We will cut on our food budget before we give up our missions giving." They both agreed.

Two days later, they received a check for $1,000 in the mail. "Surprises" such as this became a regular occurrence and ended up being a significant boost to their income while she finished her education. They remained faithful in their giving. Then God blessed her with a car.

When my oldest daughter who lives in Nashville, Tennessee, got pregnant with her first child, she and her husband were very concerned about how they were going to pay for disposable diapers. They decided the only way they could afford to pay for the disposable diapers was for him to take on a second part-time job, delivering pizzas or something of that nature.

They decided to put him in cloth diapers. The grandmother in me was trying to figure out how I could help them get some disposable diapers. Maybe $25 a week. (Have you priced them lately!!!)

I asked them to consider God's role in their lives. I told them that if they prayed God would provide for their needs supernaturally without him taking a second job. The next day I received a phone call from someone I knew (who happened to live in Nashville). She asked me if my daughter needed any diapers!

Then the following day my daughter's doorbell rang and when she opened the door her whole front porch was covered in boxes of disposable diapers. My daughter and her husband were given, absolutely without charge, enough diapers in all sizes to take care of both of their first two children! God is so good!

If they had cut back on their giving, that check would never have come in through the mail and the other blessings would not have arrived!

Another daughter wanted a particular laptop computer. She prayed specifically for what she wanted and seeded for it by name. She received the money in the mail from an unexpected source and bought her computer the next week.

Years ago when our family was torn apart and everything was lost, I went to my accountant. He examined my finances carefully, turned to me and said, "You need to stop tithing and giving all these offerings. Plan on filing bankruptcy."

I said, "Thank you very much." As I walked out, I quickly cut off those negative words and hired a new accountant who knew and agreed with the Word of God.

God is so awesome as He restores people. He has promised you His prosperity. Perhaps you have believed for His provision, but the manifestation of the increase did not come to pass when you expected it to arrive. The enemy knows what you will do with that increase and tries to block your blessings. But God also knows what you will do with that bonus, that raise, or that gift.

Your positive words spoken in faith will open the windows of heaven and His blessings will pour out over you in abundance over and above anything you can hope or think.

And my God shall supply all your need.
(Philippians 4:19)

Needs include things like transportation, housing, food, utilities, clothing, and a job to provide an income. Jesus told us not to worry about these things.

"Which of you by worrying can add one cubit to his stature? So why do you worry about clothing? Consider the lilies of the field, how they grow: they neither toil nor spin; and yet I say to you that even Solomon in all his glory was not arrayed like one of these."
(Matthew 6:27-29)

When considering your needs, the worst thing to do is to slip into fear that can lead to panic. I saw a great cartoon about this subject.

A man is sitting at a desk with sweat pouring down his forehead. The adding machine tape was dangling down into a pile all over the floor. Bills were stacked up around the room. He was in a panic. Shaking his pencil, he said, "What am I going to do?"

Just then two sparrows land on the windowsill. One says to the other, "I guess God doesn't care about him as much as He cares about us!"

I like sparrows, but I know I am more important to God than the sparrow. God says He will supply my every need. He will do the same thing for you. You are much more important and valuable than a sparrow.

Give According to a Specific Scripture

Earlier, I briefly mentioned seeding toward things by name. What I call "scriptural giving" is one of the most powerful giving tools that I know of.

Let me explain what I mean by scriptural giving. Do you know someone in the military or a missionary located in a dangerous territory somewhere around the world? Psalm 91 is a powerful Scripture about protection. My friend seeded $91.00 for his son-in-law's safety based on Psalm 91. What happened is very interesting.

This young man's job in the military required that he work with jet fuel. One day a fuel container burst and doused him with gasoline.

His wife happened to be at my house during this period of time. They had agreed on a particular hour when he would contact her by phone. The appointed time came and passed. He didn't call, he didn't call, and he didn't call. She became very worried.

Communication during the war these days is so different compared to what it used to be. Normally, her husband was able to call every day on a cell phone, not to mention e-mail or video chatting. When she did not hear from him, her anxiety manifested to panic level.

After being doused with the fuel, the young man was put in a shower and scrubbed with iron bristles from the top of his head to the soles of his feet. To save his life, the doctors put him in a drug-induced coma, feeding him intravenously to flush the poisons out of his body. On top of all that, the fuel had blinded him.

When he finally was able to call his wife to explain what happened, I said, "Father, this young man's mother-in-law seeded $91.00 for his protection and this situation does not line up with your Word. I speak his eyesight be restored. And I command anything bad that has happened because of this accident to go." His eyes opened up immediately! His sight was restored! Glory to God!

Prayers do get answered long distance on a cell phone. Don't ever limit Him!

Many of you might find Isaiah 49:25 helpful, *"And I will save your children."* If you have a child that is not serving God, seed $49.25 and stand on this promise.

You cannot buy salvation – I know that. However, you can add fuel to the fire by seeding for what you are praying and believing for. You place your loved ones on God's altar and believe for a miracle. Seeding specifically just adds more fire to your faith and prayers.

I have instructed people to plant a seed specifically for the salvation, recommitment, and/or restoration of a prodigal child. Soon after, the child they prayed for walked down the aisle of the church, dedicating their life to Jesus. This has happened hundreds of times.

People have heard me share about scriptural giving and have made it their number *one* strategy for their giving. Many people have acted upon this word by seeding $111, some seed

$111.11 a month. This comes from the following verse.

> *May the LORD God of your fathers*
> *make you a thousand times*
> *more numerous than you are,*
> *and bless you as he has promised you!*
> (Deuteronomy 1:11)

These people are receiving so much in return that they can hardly get their seed back into the ground before God blesses them again. Seed $111.11, $1,111.11, or any variation of 11. Whatever you can do, just do it, even if it's $11.11. Ask God how much to give and where to put the decimal.

Remember, you are seeding and coming into alignment with a specific Scripture verse. If you are believing God for protection, seed $91.00! If you do not have $91.00, then give $9.10 or $.91.

Understand, I am not telling you to give it to Joan Hunter Ministries; however, I am instructing you to give it to God. Ask Him where to give and God will tell you exactly where to plant your seed. Find the Scripture verse that fits your need. You may even find more than one verse. Stand on His Word. His Word is His promise. Give to

Him in faith and the circumstance you are seeding for will line up with the verse of Scripture.

> *"No weapon formed against you shall prosper,*
> *and every tongue which rises against you*
> *in judgment you shall condemn. This is the*
> *heritage of the servants of the Lord, and their*
> *righteousness is from Me," says the Lord.*
> (Isaiah 54:17)

If you are in a situation where people are
coming against you, turn to Isaiah 54:17 and seed
$54.17 as you repeat the words: *"No weapon
formed against me shall prosper."* Hallelujah!

Isaiah 49:25 is also very good to stand on if
somebody comes after you either verbally or
with a legal situation. Seed $49.25 and watch the
situation turn around.

> *But thus says the LORD…"For I will*
> *contend with him who contends with you,*
> *and I will save your children."*
> (Isaiah 49:25)

I instructed a couple to give a $49.25 seed
for a son who was separated from his wife. They
are now reunited and doing great. God is so
amazing.

This principle has always worked for me. If it works for me, it will work for you. The success I have witnessed and experienced gives me great fervency about giving scripturally. If you want to give $100.00, add Psalm 100 to it as fertilizer to stimulate its coming to fruition. Find some way to align your seed with the Word of God.

Scriptural giving will primarily be your *offering*, not the regular *tithe* of your income. Seed your offering and watch what God does.

Here are some more ideas for you. If you want greater wisdom and revelation, seed $117.19 based on the following verses.

> *That the God of our Lord Jesus Christ, the Father of glory, may give to you the spirit of wisdom and revelation in the knowledge of Him, the eyes of your understanding being enlightened; that you may know what is the hope of His calling, what are the riches of the glory of His inheritance in the saints, and what is the exceeding greatness of His power toward us who believe, according to the working of His mighty power."*
> (Ephesians 1:17-19)

If you are believing for a spouse, then seed $31.00 in line with Proverbs 31.

Another Scripture verse I like is Isaiah 55:11.

So shall my word be that goes forth out
of my mouth. It shall not return to me void,
but it shall accomplish what I please,
and it shall prosper in the thing for
which I sent it."
(Isaiah 55:11)

The Bible says that God's Word shall not return void. According to this verse, prepare whatever God has spoken to you, name your seed, plant it in good soil, and wait in faith. His promises are not wasted words. Your seed will return a harvest. It will come back to you supernaturally.

Whatever your situation is right now, you need to ask before you plant any seed, "God, first, how much do You want me to give?" If the amount He gives you does not have a scriptural reference, do not worry about it. Agree and give whatever He says. However, if you believe God for a specific situation, search the Scriptures for a verse you can stand on. Line up your offering with the verse from His Word and give the scriptural amount.

Use God's Keys to Release your Blessing

God's Kingdom does not come to just anyone. There are keys to release it into your life that help you align yourself with God's purposed blessings.

Here are the most important keys that I have discovered:

#1: Repentance is the main key to opening up the windows of heaven.

Repent for any foolish spending. Repent for any instance you have not tithed. Repent for any time you refused to give an offering when God told you to – not when an evangelist told you to give, but when God told you to give an offering and you did not obey. Disobedience is sin.

Even when you think you cannot afford to give, God will tell you what and how much to give because He wants to bless you. When the blessings start, you will know they are directly from Him.

Repeat this prayer aloud...you will be seeing it as you read and hearing it as you speak.

"Father, I repent for all foolish spending. I repent for any time I have not tithed. I repent for any time I did not obey when You told me to give an offering. All of that is sin. Take that sin from me now and put it on the cross of Jesus Christ, never to be held against me again. Father, I promise from this day to be careful with how I spend my money and to be faithful with my tithes and the offerings you tell me to give. In Jesus' name, Amen."

After today, you will be held to a higher level of accountability with your finances because you have heard the truth. When you understand this principle, you will be set free from financial burdens.

God knows when you turn from your wicked ways, such as not giving. Suddenly, miracles and blessings will appear around you. Your body may be healed. Your finances will increase. All types of incredible blessings will rain down around you.

Some people have had money show up in their bank accounts. They questioned it the first time; but when it happened again, they simply said, "Thank You, Jesus!"

What would you do if extra money just appeared in your account?

#2: Be a blessing.

God wants us to be a river for finances; however, the river has banks. The water is guided down a path. We are not to be a reservoir and hold it forever. Yes, we can have a savings account; however, we are not to hoard our blessings. We must allow His blessings flow through us to others as He directs.

Be aware that the enemy might try to give you curses disguised as blessings. Perhaps you receive a pre-approved credit card for $5,000 credit. Do not jump up and down and praise God. This is not a blessing from God. Credit is pure debt and a river cannot flow from the place of debt. A river in debt is a desert.

Often people use a credit card to purchase non-essentials and then are burdened down trying to pay off the bill. That card is not from God! It is pure temptation from the enemy.

The blessings from God are running and overtaking me wherever I go. God knows exactly where I am at all times and can send the blessings to me anywhere in the world. He knows where you are also. He also has a sense of humor and can bless you in the most surprising ways.

God is resurrecting some of the money that has been lost through the years. People who have owed you money for years will start paying you what they owe towards these old debts.

God is very creative in the ways He blesses us. However, no matter how His blessings arrive, remember that you are blessed to be a blessing, not to hoard it all for yourself. God wants you to have nice "things" as long as the things do not have you. Kelley and I have a beautiful home, but it does not keep me from travelling and doing what God has called me to do. Occasionally, I actually get to sleep there.

#3: Do not agree with the spirit of poverty.

Break off the spirit of poverty by not agreeing with it anymore. Do not let negative words come out of your mouth. Instead, choose to speak positive words.

Let them shout for joy and be glad,
who favor my righteous cause; And let
them say continually, "Let the LORD be
magnified, who has pleasure in the
prosperity of His servant."
(Psalms 35:27)

God does not say He takes pleasure in our poverty, our hunger, or our humility in being poor. He says He takes pleasure in our prosperity!

Have you heard someone say, "God is going to humble me by making me poor"? I have. Is that in agreement with His Word? No. You should be humble without having to lose everything in your life.

Receive Your Promised Inheritance

When does a person receive an inheritance? When my mom went home to be with the Lord, I inherited her necklace. When my mom died, she did not receive *her* inheritance; I received *my* inheritance.

I went to the bank a few years ago to get some information that I needed. A personal banker sitting at the desk asked, "What do you need"? I answered, "I am with Joan Hunter Ministries and I need some assistance."

She said, "I will be with you in a moment." The woman she was helping finished her business and got up to leave. She was an elderly little lady about 75 years old. She appeared to be so tired, totally drained, and heavy with sorrow.

I approached her and said, "May I pray with you? May I give you a hug?"

She said, "Yes," and I gave her a hug. She then asked me for a ride home and I agreed to take her. On the way home, she said, "You're so sweet honey. I know you don't have any idea of what it means to be betrayed."

She looked a bit surprised when I said, "Yes I do. I even wrote a book about what happened to me." I had a copy of my book *Healing the Heart* in the car, so I gave it to her.

She told me that her husband had died seven years before. They lived in a very nice home, but she lost everything after he died. Only two weeks before we met, she discovered that her husband had died a multi-millionaire.

At the time she made this discovery, she was living below the poverty line. She was extremely upset because the executor of the will had withheld all her inheritance. Her husband's business partner and best friend had kept it all for himself.

This is a tragic story because of the injustice this woman suffered when her inheritance was withheld from her. The reason I tell you this story is to ask you this question: Who is holding back your inheritance?

When Jesus Christ died, you received your inheritance. You are not waiting to receive it at some future date. It is there for you to claim.

Part of your inheritance is the anointing of the Holy Spirit, the power of the blood of Jesus over evil, peace, all of His authority and an abundant life.

All of your needs are met in Christ Jesus. This is your inheritance, already given to you, and it is a tragedy to suffer the injustice of it being withheld from you!

When difficult situations come against me I say, "You are trespassing, you must leave in Jesus' name."

You have to reach the point where you are not going to put up with it anymore. You have had enough. The enemy has taken enough. It is past the time for life and restoration. Kick the enemy out of your life and off your finances.

When God restores, He always returns at least seven times what was stolen by the enemy. The next time you give an offering for a specific need, declare these verses over your gift:

> *Give, and it will be given to you: good meas-*
> *ure, pressed down, shaken together, and run-*
> *ning over will be put into your bosom.*
> (Luke 6:38)

When you send out your seed offering with God's Word for a specific purpose, it will come back to you having accomplished everything it was sent to do (Isaiah 55:11).

Remove Hindrances to Receiving

It is time for your blessing and inheritance to break through! It will not tarry!

> *Then the Lord answered me and said,*
> *"Write the vision and make it plain on*
> *tablets that he may run who reads it.*
> *The vision is yet for an appointed time,*
> *it will not tarry. It will surely come."*
> (Habakkuk 2:2)

If God has given you a vision and you have made it plain to others, then you are now at the point of "NO MORE DELAY!" Things have been held back from you, but it is time for things to move forward. Deal with the hindering forces and walk in all God has for you. He wants to supernaturally bless you. I cannot repeat this statement often enough!

There was a particular place where I wanted to minister. They told me they had wanted me to minister there for over two years. This place was also one of my favorite places to visit. I came against the hindering forces that were keeping that meeting date from coming to pass. A few minutes later, I received an e-mail requesting a date. Hallelujah! God was giving me this revelation about hindering forces and teaching me how to pray against them for this specific need.

***

I believe the more specific we pray,

the better the results we receive.

***

A little boy fell and hurt his head while playing. His mother put her hand on his shoulder to pray. He took her hand and put it on his head and said, "No, Mommy, my shoulder doesn't hurt; my head hurts." Even a four year old understood that his mom needed to have her hand in the right place when she prayed.

When you pray for your finances, be specific. Like the boy told his mother, ask God to put His hand where it hurts. Don't stop with, "Father, bless my finances!" Instead say:

> "Father, I declare that I have more than enough finances in my account to meet all my needs! Father, I am so glad I can give You more than just a 10 percent tithe. Father, I can freely give whenever and wherever You tell me to give. I am a radical giver. Thank You for all Your blessings."

Believe It's God's Desire to Bless You

God wants you to be blessed. When one of my children gets a raise, do I say something like, "OH NO, it is terrible that you got a raise!!"? Absolutely not! I cheer and yell! God is so awesome! It is a time of rejoicing!

You are blessed to be a blessing. You are not blessed to hoard. Right now God wants you to get into alignment with the Word so He can open the windows of heaven and pour out His blessings.

Here is something fun you can do. Add up everything you owe. Why? To make you feel bad? No! You never know when someone might walk up to you and ask, "How much do you owe? I want to write a check right now to pay off all your debts!" Could you answer them? Be prepared. Plan on it happening to you! Include your mortgage, your car loan, and your credit card liabilities. Expect it!

A woman was depending on child support from her ex-husband. When he was arrested and imprisoned, all support stopped. In order to feed her children, she used credit cards. One day, someone contacted her and informed her he wanted to pay off her credit cards. She was prepared to receive God's blessings. God supplied over and abundantly to meet her needs. God used one of his relatives.

While we are on the subject of the blessings that come on single parents, I want to tell you of another blessing that happened to a friend of mine.

She has a teenage daughter, and that in itself can be expensive. She has done well in the provision of her child with some help from her ex-husband. She was believing for an extra amount of money to help her during the month of December. She seeded for a blessing. Her ex-husband got a substantial bonus on his job and gave her the ENTIRE bonus check!!! That HAS to be God!!!

Do not look to the natural for your blessing. God is your Provider and He will supernaturally send finances into your life. He can move on anyone, anytime, anywhere to bless you! He takes pleasure in your prosperity and knows exactly where and when and how the money will arrive.

When we left Kingwood to move to Pine-hurst, only a few people knew where we had moved. However, my God knew exactly where I was! Unexpected money came in at our new home.

This is powerful. I want you to understand, know, and walk in this revelation. If I had not experienced this revelation in my own life, I could not share this testimony with anyone. But I have experienced it.

I can still vividly recall the heartache when there was no money for food for my children in 2000. I still remember the tears of joy when God supernaturally blessed us and supplied just what we needed right at the moment we needed it most.

Pray right now:

"Father, in the name of Jesus, I thank you that the seeds I have planted in good soil are going to come up quickly in Jesus' name because I am fertilizing it with the Word of God."

When you go to the mailbox, say: "Father, I am excited about what you are going to send."

If there is something in your mailbox, say, "Praise God!"

If there isn't anything, say, "Not today," or, "Not yet, but it is coming." Don't be negative. Expect! Expect! Expect!

He will get it to you

if He can get it through you!

God wants to bless you! Plan for His blessings! Open a savings account. Be ready to handle all the money when it comes. In the natural, one plus one equals two. In the perfect alignment of God, 1 and 1 equals 11.

Know Who Your Father Is

A friend of mine is a security guard. People hire him to protect them when they travel and he has travelled widely. On one occasion, he was hired to escort two princes from a foreign country and provide their security while they were in the United States.

He met their plane and stayed with them around the clock. They all checked into a very nice hotel that charged several thousand dollars a night per room. They always use credit cards that have no limit. Then they would have dinner and go to various bars.

I said to my friend, "That must have been horrible for you." He replied, "No, it wasn't. It was one of the most incredible experiences I've ever had."

He continued to explain. The princes and their entourage would fly from Texas to California just to have lunch and then fly back that night. These princes always did whatever they wanted to do and never worried about not having enough money. They never worried about paying their bills or having a place to sleep at night. They always held their heads up high and their shoulders back because they knew who their father was.

Most of us cannot relate to that kind of lifestyle. However, we need to realize that we can and should live with that level of confidence because we know who our Father is. Our Father is much more important than the father of those princes.

We should hold our heads up high. Our Father is the King of Kings and Lord of Lords. We should not worry about where our next meal is going to come from or where we will sleep. Our "Daddy" will provide from His abundance for His obedient kids, you and me!

Jesus said:

"Therefore I say to you, do not worry about your life, what you will eat or what you will drink; nor about your body, what you will put on. Is not life more than food and the body more than clothing? Look at the birds of the air, for they neither sow nor reap nor gather into barns; yet your heavenly Father feeds them. Are you not of more value than they? Which of you by worrying can add one cubit to his stature? So why do you worry about clothing? Consider the lilies of the field, how they grow: they neither toil nor spin; and yet I say to you that even Solomon in all his glory was not arrayed like one of these. Now if God so clothes the grass of the field, which today is, and tomorrow is thrown into the oven, will He not much more clothe you, O you of little faith? Therefore do not worry, saying, 'What shall we eat?' or 'What shall we drink?' or 'What shall we wear?' For after all these things the Gentiles seek. For your heavenly Father knows that you need all these things. But seek first the kingdom of God and His righteousness, and all these things shall be added to you."

(Matthew 6:25-33)

In God's kingdom, when you are faithful with little and He knows He can trust you with a small assignment, He will then add more important responsibilities. You will be made a ruler over much. You will be promoted.

God made us in His image. We share His attributes. Every time we meet a new person or learn a new concept, we evaluate a person's honesty or test the new idea. When we understand and believe the person is honorable or the concept is true, our belief grows stronger.

As baby Christians, we also "test" God just as He instructs us to do. Children do the same with their parents. Are you ready to "prove" God?

"Bring all the tithes into the storehouse,
that there may be food in my house,
and try me now in this," says the LORD
of hosts, "If I will not open for you the
windows of heaven and pour out for
you such blessing that there will not be
room enough to receive it."
(Malachi 3:10)

God has already given you seeds to sow. Seeds do not have to be in the form of money in every instance. If you think you don't have any "seed" to sow, give a compact, a button or a pen in the offering. Maybe you have time to volunteer to meet a need at church that is right in line with your talents. He will use the talents He has blessed you with and will open those doors.

Watch and expect opportunities to give to Him in unique ways. God wants to bless your socks off. He is going to free you up to do what He has called you to do.

If I am worrying and fretting about finances, I cannot do what God has called me to do. "What am I going to do? How am I going to pay for this? I cannot go minister around the world because it is so expensive. I'll just sit in my house and worry about how to pay the ministry employees!"

Do I do that? Oh, NO! It is up to God to take care of the needs of this ministry and I am not going to worry or attempt to do God's part. He tells me when and where and how much seed to sow. I do my part when I sow scripturally according to an appropriate Scripture verse.

What is next? I trust God. He always comes through. Unlike some humans, He keeps His promises. Maybe not always in my timing, but He does keep His Word in His perfect timing.

God wants to pour out the blessings of heaven in every area of your life. Are you ready? Are you prepared to sow? Are you prepared to receive? Are your barns built and ready to receive His overwhelming harvest of blessings? Okay, maybe you do not want a barn. Do you have a savings account ready and waiting?

Experience the Power of Obedience

It is so easy to pray and ask God for a quick fix in any given situation. You pray and ask God to move on your behalf without even a thought. You boldly ask God to move mountains and expect them to disappear. His Word does tell you to do this and you are to obediently follow His instructions. You then fully expect His instant response to your every request.

But let me ask you a question. How fast have you responded when God has asked you to do something? How quick are you to listen to the still small voice of His Holy Spirit? How often is complete obedience your first choice? How long does God have to wait until you obey His request?

Parents know the importance of complete obedience. When a parent tells a child to pick up their toys, make their beds, or finish their homework, the parent expects obedience within a short period of time. However, a parent can get very upset with the child if they do not do what is expected until the next week. Grumbling, moaning, and groaning as the child follows the orders is a common rebellious response accompanying this type of obedience.

When God asks you, His child, to do something, He expects you to respond with obedience to do what is asked of you without mumbling or grumbling. God does not like the rebellious complaining from His children any more than an earthly parent does.

✱✱✱

How quickly and willingly

do we respond to Him?

✱✱✱

God has commanded you to bring the tithe, (10 percent of your income) into the storehouse where you are fed spiritually. Why? So there will be food in the house of God. When everyone contributes their part, there is plenty of resources to accomplish the work of God.

I believe there are two reasons for the tithe, one that is natural and one that is supernatural. The natural reason is the actual physical needs, like paying the water and electric bill, staff salaries, outreach events, facility upkeep and supplies, etc. These things are necessary in today's society. You like going to a place with the lights on, the sound system working, and the water connected in the bathrooms and water fountains.

The supernatural reason for the tithe is for your benefit – the blessing that comes from your obedience.

> *"Test me in this, see if I will not throw open the floodgates of heaven and pour out so much blessing that you will not have room for it."*
> (Malachi 3:10)

He is making you a promise. When you tithe 10 percent, God multiplies the 90 percent that is left to meet your needs. He wants your obedience. It proves that you worship Him and not your money.

Going a step further, the Holy Spirit will tell you to give an offering – an amount above or in addition to your tithe. He is giving you one more opportunity to give to Him in obedience and remind yourselves that you trust God with all that you have. Regardless of what uncertainties you have, you know and can be sure that God can do more with your money than you can.

It has been said time and time again, "If it is not enough to meet your need, it must be your seed." You plant your seed by sowing it when and where God tells you to plant it. Seeds planted in your garden grow into plants or vegetables.

Financial seeds sowed or planted into the supernatural reap finances in the natural. It is not a get rich quick scheme; it is how God blesses obedience. God is after your heart, not your money! Regardless of what you give, when you are giving in obedience to God, He will bless you in return.

Several years ago, a family volunteered to work with Mom and Dad. During one of their meetings, two of their children volunteered to watch some small children while the parents enjoyed the services. When the children were picked up, my parents blessed the two girls with some money.

Surprised, they immediately took the gift to their parents. When asked what they wanted to do with this unexpected gift, the girls agreed they wanted to give it all to God. They seeded that money into Mom and Dad's ministry.

The following day at the motel where they were staying, an older lady came up to them at the pool and said, "I don't get to see my grandchildren very often. You two look like such nice girls that I want to give you something." She pulled out two $20 bills and gave one to each of the speechless girls.

They came running down the hall to share their "miracle" with the family. "It works! It works! God multiplied our $2!!"

They have never forgotten their first experience of giving all they had to a loving Father and receiving His multiplied blessings. Need I go further to say they quickly planted that seed of $20 into good soil again and again through the years?

Receive the Promises of Obedience

Deuteronomy 28 is a great chapter in the Bible. It spends the first third of the chapter explaining the blessings that come if we *"diligently obey the voice of the LORD your God"* (verse 1). Verse 2 goes on to say, *"These blessings shall come upon you and overtake you."*

These blessings are a guarantee for those who *"keep the commandments of the LORD your God and walk in His ways."*

These are the blessings God promises you when you obey Him:

1. He sets you high above all nations of the earth (God gives you favor that differentiates you from others).

2. You will be blessed in the city and in the country in both selling and producing your goods. This includes the fruit of your body – children, a legacy that continues the work God has given to you, the produce of your ground, the increase of your herds and your cattle, the offspring of your flocks, your basket and your kneading bowl. (In other words, you will have great success in all you do.)

3. You will be blessed going out and coming in (as you enter and exit no matter where you go).

4. All your enemies are and will be defeated (you win!).

5. Your storehouses are blessed. (This includes resources and investments gain, increase in value and do not shrink!)

6. You are established as a holy people unto God whom the nations fear. (The world knows you belong to God and the only way they win is by blessing you!)

7. You will receive plenty of goods, the opening of God's good treasure, and the heavens to give you rain for your land in its season. (He blesses all the work of your hand, increasing business and resources, providing in seasons when you need it most.)

8. You will lend and not borrow; you are the head and not the tail; you shall be above only, and not be beneath. (This includes prosperity, increase, blessings on your work, lending and not borrowing, leading our industries, only increasing always.)

God is not limited by the industrial and technological revolutions and is well able to bless you today in ways that are relevant to your modern way of life.

There is nothing that can harm you because there is provision and protection in obedience. Malachi explains that just giving the tithe will open the windows of heaven. So if the windows of heaven are open, blessings are coming to you straight from God. Blessings may come in the form of a promotion at work, a bonus, someone treating you to lunch, paying for your gas, etc.

God will use people in your life to bless you. You just need to recognize that it is not just that person blessing you, but God putting it on their heart to bless you.

It is natural to desire only good things to happen in your life. You do not wake up in the morning saying, "I hope I get a flat tire on the way to work, after spilling hot coffee on my new shirt and oversleeping after missing my alarm."

You do not think that way. You hope for all green lights on the way to work and no traffic on the freeway. And however the lights change or how crowded the freeway is, you accept those things as part of life and can be thankful for God's timing, protection, and accident prevention.

Avoid the Curses of Disobedience

Now just as there are promises of blessing when you obey God, there are warnings and consequences that come from disobedience. These are not to be taken lightly.

Malachi explained the giving of tithes opens the windows of heaven. Have you ever wondered what happens if you do not tithe? Very simply, the opposite occurs. Not obeying God closes the windows of heaven. Rebellion to God's direction locks those windows.

★★★

Disobedience is the deadbolt

on the windows of heaven.

★★★

You may think to yourself that not tithing is not rebellion, but it is rebellion. You are choosing to do the opposite of what God has instructed you to do. It is the same as you telling your children to make their bed and they choose not to do it. Unfortunately, the consequences for not tithing are much more severe than when a child refuses to make their bed.

We are clearly warned in Deuteronomy 28:15-68 about the consequences of disobedience. Wow! Fifty-four verses! In each of the ways God blesses if you obey, you will be cursed if you disobey.

On top of that, these curses will come upon you and overtake you:

1. Cursing, confusion, and rebuke in all that you set your hand to do until you are destroyed and until you perish quickly.

2. The plague will cling to you until it has consumed you from the land that you are going to possess.

3. Your enemies will pursue you until you perish, the heavens over your head shall be bronze, and the earth under you shall be iron.

4. The LORD will change the rain of your land to powder and dust; from the heaven it shall come down on you until you are destroyed.

5. You will develop boils, tumors, scabs, and the itch from which you cannot be healed.

6. You will experience madness, blindness, and confusion of heart.

7. You shall grope at noonday, as a blind man gropes in darkness.

8. You shall not prosper in your ways. You shall be only oppressed and plundered continually, and no one shall save you.

9. You will have an unfaithful spouse and business partners.

10. There will be stealing, killing, and destroying all around you personally and professionally.

11. There will be captivity and bondage in life.

12. You will work hard but profit little.

13. Others will rise higher and higher above you, and you shall come down lower and lower.

14. You will borrow and not lend; you will be the tail and not the head.

15. You will experience hunger, thirst, nakedness, and be in need of everything.

16. Opposition, disrespect, dishonor and complete destruction will come upon you.

17. There will be extraordinary plagues – great and prolonged plagues – and serious and prolonged sicknesses to you and the generation that follows you.

18. Lack and decrease will appear on all sides.

19. You will be brought to nothing and plucked from off the land which you go to possess.

20. You will be scattered all over the earth.

21. You will serve other gods.

22. You will find no place to rest.

23. You will have a trembling heart, failing eyes, and anguish of soul.

24. Your life shall hang in doubt before you; you shall fear day and night, and have no assurance of life. In the morning you shall say, "Oh, that it were evening!" And at evening you shall say, "Oh, that it were morning!" because of the fear which terrifies your heart, and because of the sight which your eyes see.

25. You will be offered for sale to your enemies, but no one will buy you.

You may wonder why I included so much of Deuteronomy 28. I cannot tell you only the good things included in this chapter. It is important for you to know what the Word of God says concerning you…both good and bad.

More than that, this is not information you are likely to find in a devotional. The second part of chapter 28 is not something most people would choose to read to start your day.

Do not allow fear to start. Keep reading.

When you are in obedience and listening to the Holy Spirit, the second part of this chapter does not apply to your life. It becomes null and void. The Bible says several times that *if* you listen and obey what God has commanded, disease and destruction will not affect you or your life.

Your life is filled with daily opportunities for stress to enter. You are susceptible to even more stress if you are worried about paying your bills on time, the children needing clothes, or loans and other payments are due? Life has a way of becoming overwhelming if you let things get out of line.

When your tithes and offerings are not remembered or given, your lives are out of alignment. You start looking to your boss, birthday money, holiday bonuses and anniversaries as a way to make ends meet. Instead, you should have been maintaining your focus and priorities of keeping God first and your tithe given in a timely manner.

Follow the Promptings
of the Holy Spirit

The Holy Spirit speaks to each person in His own way. For you, it may be as simple as acknowledging that your thought has come from Him and not from your own mind. Whether you are in church or at lunch with friends, He can speak to you. He is not limited by your environment or conversation unless you have made Him unwelcome.

The Holy Spirit is the One who speaks to you about offerings. He is the One who quickens your spirit and makes your heart race just a little bit. He is your guide for the natural steps you take in your life.

God directs your path and the Holy Spirit is like your navigational system helping you find the right road. He is like your own personal GPS leading you to your destination. The Holy Spirit nudges your heart when you hear about missions, outreaches, and ministries needing support.

He speaks to you in that still small voice and tells you what to give and how you can help. From that moment on, it is up to you to obey. You need to follow what He has told you to do and when He has told you to do it. If there is any form of compromise or delay in obedience, your inaction is disobedience.

What do I mean by compromise or delay? If the Holy Spirit directs you to give $100 and you give $25 with the mental promise of sending the remaining $75, you have just created compromise and delay. By this seemingly simple action, you have invited the curse of disobedience into your life.

Also, if the Holy Spirit puts it on your heart to give $25 and you give $100, it is still disobedience. You are His sheep and His sheep know His voice. So regardless of the amount you are told to give or where to serve or how to help, complete obedience should always be your focus.

***

God is not after your money,

He is after your heart!

***

God wants you to be obedient the first time He tells you to do something. He is your Heavenly Father who only wants the best for you.

Every good gift and every perfect gift is from above, and comes down from the Father of lights, with whom there is no variation or shadow of turning.
(James 1:17)

He is the same yesterday, today and tomorrow and He does not change regardless of what is going on in the world.

When you are in complete obedience, you are in the perfect will of God. It is impossible to be disobedient and yet still be doing what God has called you to do.

So now that you know and have a full understanding of how important obedience is, you must make every effort to do all that God asks of you.

Pray For Breakthrough!

Now that we have discussed the keys to breakthrough in your finances, I am going to lead you to pray over several things. It if pertains to you, pray it. Pray by name. Be specific. Hindering forces need to be gone.

You are going to pray over commission jobs, break the spirit of poverty, declare pay raises, bonuses, and donations to support what God has given you to do. Hindering forces have stopped the finances from coming in. So be specific. Name your need. Do you need a physical healing? Call it by name. Could you use more finances? Say exactly where or what the need is.

I want your finances healed. I want everyone to be able to give millions of dollars to further God's work. I want God's windows of heaven to be thrown open wide and allow His abundance of prosperity overwhelm you in every area of your life.

Do you need to find the perfect spouse God has prepared for you? Do you need to grow into the spouse your husband or wife needs?

Let me pray for you as we begin: "Father, I agree with Your will for this person's life and come against any hindering spirits blocking the full release of Your blessings, in Jesus' name."

Now roll up your sleeves and put on your fighting gloves. Pray each prayer aloud wherever the subject fits your specific need. Remember to pray these prayers out loud. You will see the words, read the words and hear the words as you speak them.

If someone owes you money, pray:

"Father, I thank You in Jesus name, that any money owed to me will be restored now. In the name of Jesus, I ask You to move on (<u>insert the person's name</u>) heart that they will pay me the money they owe me. Bless them."

After sitting in one of my services and praying this prayer, a woman was on her way home from church. Her husband called to tell her a $13,000 check had arrived to pay off a 15 year-old debt!

If you work a commission sales job, pray:

"Father, You know I am on commission. Any hindering forces that would cause people not to buy are gone now in Jesus' name. I speak jobs and sales and my commission to increase supernaturally in Jesus' name."

If you want an increase in pay and bonuses:

"Father, I believe you want to bless and prosper me, so whether I have been promised a pay raise or not, I speak a pay raise into my finances. I speak bonuses into my life in Jesus' name."

If you desire or need a different job:

"Father, I thank You for the job You are going to give me. I thank You for the job that is coming quickly that will far exceed any hope, dream, or desire I have. In Jesus' name, Amen."

If you need donations or outside income to support your ministry:

"Father, I command any hindering forces against friends or ministry partners that are keeping them from giving to You and Your work, to be gone in Jesus' name. Father, I thank You that any support that has been promised is here in Jesus' name.

"(Insert person's name) has made a promise of (insert amount of money owed or promised). Father, in the name of Jesus, speak to (person's name) to fulfill their promise. Bless them, Father, so they will be able to fulfill this obligation. Father, I pray that the money will come in supernaturally this week. Move on their hearts to pay their vow. Thank you for blessing them. In Jesus' name."

If you need a home or want your home paid off this year:

"Father, in the name of Jesus, I thank You for my home and I thank You that my home mortgage is supernaturally paid off. If I do not have a home, I thank You for my home in Jesus' name."

A woman was praying for her own home. She backed up her faith by seeding specifically for her home. The city of Lincoln, Nebraska, gives away a new home every year. They pass out fifteen keys and the person holding the right key gets the home debt-free. She now lives in a beautiful home totally debt-free because her key opened the door!

Cars, whether you need one or have one:

> "Father, I need a car. I need it paid for. I thank You for supernaturally paying for it in full, in Jesus' name."

Credit card debt:

> "Father, I have credit card debt. Help me to supernaturally pay it off and keep it that way, in Jesus' name."

God will not be writing you a check, but He can use very unusual sources to get the finances into your hands. It is also important to change your habits so that you do not get yourself back in the same place once God frees you of this debt.

If you want to be pregnant or know a friend who wants to be pregnant:

> "Father, I want to be pregnant OR I have a friend or family member who is having trouble getting pregnant. I command any hindering forces to be gone in Jesus' name. I command the tubes and uterus to be open and receptive to conception and for an increase in sperm, in Jesus' name."

I prayed this prayer for my daughter and she got pregnant four days later. They had tried for over 2 ½ years.

Unsaved spouse:

"Father, whatever the hindering forces are, including myself, which are preventing my spouse from being saved. I thank You for removing them, in Jesus' name.

Unsaved children:

"Father, whatever the hindering forces are that are keeping my children from coming to You, I command them to be gone. I claim Isaiah 49:25 that says…"I will save your children." No more hindrances. No more delays, in Jesus' name."

God's gift of marriage:

"I thank you that my spouse is coming to me this year. You are speaking to me in order to prepare me for him/her. I want to be a blessing for my spouse who is already on their way into my life. Thank You, Father. In Jesus' name."

Agree with your spouse to become all you need to be for each other:

> "Father, I pray that I quickly become the man/woman of God that my spouse deserves, that I will be the husband/wife You want me to be for her/him. In Jesus' name!"

Well done! What you have just prayed has released powerful things that you will begin to experience.

Now, repeat the following phrase a number of times:

> "I am blessed to be a blessing!
>
> I am blessed to be a blessing!!
>
> I am blessed to be a blessing!!!"

You are breaking the spirit of poverty as you repeat that phrase over and over. Say it louder and louder!!

> I am blessed to be a blessing!
>
> I am blessed to be a blessing!!
>
> I am blessed to be a blessing!!!
>
> I am blessed to be a blessing!!!!

Now praise Him for His blessings!

"Father, I thank You that all Your many blessings as described in Deuteronomy are being poured all over every area of my life and overtaking me now, in Jesus name."

Commit to Give and be a Blessing

The Bible tells us a story about a few loaves of bread and some fish. I can tell you from experience that when I am speaking to a crowd in a meeting, my stomach is the last thing on my mind. In this story, Jesus is speaking to 5,000 men.

Jesus was giving and giving and giving of Himself. His adrenaline was speeding through his body. God's anointing was flowing.

Someone suddenly said, "We are getting hungry. We need something to eat." The disciples were not prepared to take care of an issue like this.

Just then, a young boy came forward with his lunch that his mom prepared for him. He gave all he had to Jesus. Jesus took the loaves and fish and held them up to God.

"Father, You see this sacrificial gift from this boy. This young man has given his all, and he is willing to go without in order for the needs of Your Kingdom be met. I hold his gift up to You. Father, I ask You to bless this food and multiply it over the next six months."

Is that what He said? No, He did not say that at all! He thanked God for multiplying the food to meet the need at that very moment.

The need was *now*. Just like Jesus' disciples, your need is *now*. You need *now* provision, *now* debt paid off, *now* salvation, *now* blessings. God wants to supernaturally bless you to meet all of your needs **NOW!**

In order to open up the windows of heaven and activate the blessings of God, the one thing you need to do is give. Give something to God. Exercise your faith in His promises.

Give into good soil. Give where God tells you to plant your seed. Practice obedience and reap His blessings!

Pray this prayer aloud after you have written out a seed offering:

"Father, I lift up a loaves and fish offering. You know my need is now, even better than I know. You know what I will do with the blessings that You will pour upon me. Father, You tell me what to give and where to give. I know that I know that You will take care of all my concerns and bless every corner of my life. Amen."

Possess the Land God Has For You

Do not give up on your dreams and visions. Fulfill the destiny God has for you. If you take this revelation and live by it, you will experience the same miracles that my family and many ministry partners have enjoyed.

When someone gives you a gift, you have to receive it. You have to reach out and accept it. God is giving His blessings to you right now. His Word has explained what He wants to do for you and how you can live in His perfect will. Now it is up to you.

★★★

Reach out and receive.

★★★

Pray this prayer aloud:

"Father, in the name of Jesus, I renounce and break off the spirit of poverty. In Jesus' name, I no longer have to walk in poverty because I am going to walk in prosperity according to Your Word. I will walk in prosperity not only in my finances, but also in every area of my life. Father, I have the mind of Christ, not a poverty mindset. All negative thinking is gone, in Jesus' name. Any fear is gone, in Jesus' name. I will be limited in my listening to and watching of the news. I will no longer allow the opinions of man to be my god of direction. I am going to turn to Your Word for divine direction, and I am blessed to be a blessing! In Jesus' name. Amen!"

Testimonies
To Build Your Faith

Testimonies about financial miracles arrive in our ministry office daily. Miracle babies are being born, healings are happening. Some days, it is hard to keep up with them all. I have chosen some representative testimonies to include here. Remember, these blessings are coming to every-day people from all walks of life…and from all over the world.

Enjoy reading about these miracles. Feel the excitement coming through their words. Let your faith grow and believe for your own miracles. Don't forget to write me about what happens in your home and family (info@joanhunter.org).

God delights in the prosperity of His saints. God wants us to prosper. IT IS HIS WILL FOR US TO PROSPER!

****

A young woman listened to this teaching, an within a short period of time, she learned that a $1,500 debt that she owed was totally FORGIVEN. Later, she was called into her boss's office. The company had been laying off people for the previous few months and she thought she was next. Instead of being fired, she received a promotion and a raise!

✱✱✱✱

A couple from Mesa, AZ, came to my conference in Albuquerque, NM. When they got home, the babysitter they had hired to watch their five children refused to accept the $200 they wanted to pay her.

The miracle continued. They were closing on a house in the near future and they had money in their safe in preparation for that day. Getting ready for closing, they went to the safe to double check the amount they had so carefully saved. There was $2,700 MORE than what their records showed! They were so excited at what God had done. A few days later, they counted it AGAIN to be sure they had counted correctly. This time the total was $3,200 MORE. They called me immediately and we rejoiced together.

✱✱✱✱

"During one of your services in Ohio, you mentioned that we would be hearing about full ride college scholarships. About 1 ½ months ago, my married son received a call from a university asking him if he was interested in getting his Master's Degree. A year before, he had applied for a scholarship but had been denied. This phone call asked if he was still interested. They said they had made a mistake the year before in not giving it to him. They wanted to give him a second chance. He received a full ride scholarship!! I know beyond a shadow of doubt that it was God! This scholarship will be worth $50,000 to $60,000. PRAISE GOD!!!"

✯✯✯✯

A church I was ministering in gave a small amount in the offering. At the time, it was all they could afford. Someone walked in whom they had NEVER met and seeded $1,000 into the church.

✯✯✯✯

"Since becoming a partner I have seen my finances blessed beyond measure. I recently received a promotion, a SUBSTANTIAL RAISE plus bonuses, and was given more territory (the only woman ever to get any territory in this company)."

✯✯✯✯

"I was in debt – A LOT of debt. I didn't know how to get out. I came to a conference and received my "Set of Keys" and I have used ALL of them – especially the financial key. I repented and planted my seed and did GOD EVER BLESS THAT SEED!!!!!!!! I am completely out of debt. Thank You, Jesus!!!"

★★★★

"I believed to get out of debt this year. I seeded and within 2 weeks I was out of debt."

★★★★

"My husband gave me $40 to give in the offering as I left for church. Offering time came and I gave the $40 plus $12 I had in my pocket. It was all I had. Before the service was over, I received a call from my husband stating that I had received a bonus of over 100 times what I had just seeded in the offering that night."

★★★★

"I believed God for finances for some new clothes necessary for my new job. I seeded for ALL my needs to be met. The next week I received a check and a note specifically saying I was to use the money for clothes. God cares about everything that concerns us."

★★★★

"I keep reading this book over and over. It gets better and better as the message sinks in. This revelation is going to have a great impact on all who hear this message. It is AWESOME!!"

★★★★

"I prayed the hindering forces off of my son and his school work. He was chosen best in the class to go before the whole school and talk."

★★★★

"My son wanted to get into a particular preparatory school. They had turned him down several times. We listened to your teaching on 'End-time Economics,' applied what it said, and two hours later on a Saturday, they called to let us know he had been accepted."

★★★★

"We are in the real estate business and hadn't closed on anything in four months. We heard 'Endtime Economics' and prayed the prayers. That month we had five closings and more the following week. We are scheduling showings every two hours because God's windows of heaven have opened up over our business."

★★★★

"I am working around my house confessing, 'I am blessed to be a blessing!' And God's blessings are pouring in."

★★★★

"I just started a new job at a bank. My responsibility is to bring in new clients. After listening to your teaching, six new clients brought in over a million dollars to the bank in a time when no new accounts were being opened."

★★★★

"I had put a deposit down for a trip that I had to cancel. After numerous attempts to get a refund, I applied what you said. They called me the next week and have returned some of the money. The rest is coming next month! Praise God!"

★★★★

"We are in the commercial real estate business and have had many deals fall through. We spoke over each of them with the revelation of 'Endtime Economics.' These 'dead' deals have been resurrected and are coming through. Thank you for sharing your revelation on 'Endtime Economics.'"

∗∗∗∗

"Someone owed me money for over six years. After I listened to your teaching on 'End-time Economics,' I received a phone call a week later and they started paying me back."

∗∗∗∗

"I needed a new truck and I am believing for a new job which requires special training. I listened to your teaching. Then I wrote down my goals and all I am believing for. The next day a miracle truck came across my path. It is now mine! Paid for in full! ALSO, the next day the school opened up for me to get certified for my new job."

∗∗∗∗

"I got back more from the IRS this year than last year. And I gave into the Kingdom more than two times what I got back last year. The more I give the more I receive. God can trust me with His increase. This is not bragging on me, it is bragging on HIM!!!"

∗∗∗∗

"We gave a sacrificial gift of $5 in your service last week. Before we left the meeting, God told someone to give us a check for five hundred dollars...the exact amount we were believing for! Thank you, Jesus."

★★★★

"I needed my truck repaired. The estimate from the shop was $700. I walked around my house saying, 'I am blessed to be a blessing!' When I went to pick up my vehicle, the total read $350. When I questioned the difference, he said, 'Ma'am, someone just came in and paid half the bill!' Thank You, Jesus!"

★★★★

"I had a lawsuit pending regarding a large settlement. This situation was holding up payment of my money. I listened to your teaching and prayed those prayers. The lawsuit was dropped the next morning. Thank You, Jesus!"

★★★★

"I needed my car repaired while I was on vacation. It was going to cost $450 that was not in my budget. When I went to pick it up, the bill had been paid before I got there. Thank You Jesus!"

★★★★

"My daughter was having a hard time getting pregnant after two and a half years of trying.

I heard your teaching on 'Endtime Economics' and prayed the prayer regarding hindrances that were keeping her from getting pregnant. She got pregnant that week! Thank You, Jesus."

✦✦✦✦

"After hearing you speak on 'Endtime Economics,' I feel like I can hope again. Your teaching has been such a blessing. I feel so good to have my hope renewed and believe that prosperity is on its way!"

✦✦✦✦

A couple was believing to get out of debt quickly. A man walked up to them at church and gave them a check for $1,000 with the words "God told me to give you this!"

✦✦✦✦

My husband, Kelley, and I were hoping to get our taxes on our house lowered (with the prices of houses going down). He went to the tax assessors and presented our case. They looked at our file and said, "You are actually paying LESS per square foot than your neighbors. The homes in your area have NOT depreciated and your house is worth the same as when you bought it two years ago."

****

"I called your office to ask for prayer. My inheritance had been held up in court for years. They prayed with me and told me about 'End-time Economics' and to break any hindering forces holding it back. We prayed together and I got a call the next morning saying my inheritance had been released. Thank You, Jesus!"

****

"I got your teaching on 'Endtime Economics' and I prayed over my daughter and son-in-law to have a baby like you said to do. A few weeks later my daughter called to say she was pregnant." (There have been many of these testimonies that have come in.)

****

A lady gave all she had into the offering. Before she left the building, God had multiplied it over 100 times.

****

A woman in Ohio gave in the offering. She named the seed "Tuition scholarship for her daughter." After the offering had been received, I had a word of knowledge over the offering that two scholarships would be given to two families that gave that day (Sunday). This word saddened another woman. Her son wanted a scholarship badly but had just been turned down. On Monday the first woman receive a letter saying her daughter had been given a full scholarship. BUT God you said two! The school called the second woman's son and said they had made a mistake and gave him the scholarship. Thank You, Jesus!

★★★★

I was teaching on "Endtime Economics" and a woman reluctantly gave in the offering. "We'll just see if this works," she thought. She named it "My husband's business." When she got up to leave she looked at her phone and there were two voice mails – two jobs worth over $1 million each. She is a believer now.

★★★★

After learning about "Endtime Economics," many people have called the office to have someone agree with them over financial situations and legal situations. Many times the person will call back the next day and say that they settled out of court and they dropped the suit. We agree with them that no weapon formed against them shall prosper and that any hindering forces keeping finances from coming in be gone in Jesus' name.

****

"After hearing you talk on finances, I seeded for my school bill to be paid off. Within a month, I received notification that my $10,000 school loan had been paid in full."

****

"I gave and I named my seed, "Hospital bill to be paid for." That was on a Sunday. On Monday I got a letter from my insurance company telling me that they had decided to cover it all. $35,000!"

****

"I heard your teaching and I gave, believing that my credit card debt would be paid off and not to let it get up there again. I did what you said to do. I prayed what you said to pray. I repented. I got notification from my credit card company that they choose one person a year to forgive the debt and I was the one that year."

****

"I heard your teaching when you were in New Mexico. I prayed what you said to pray. I had no job and no prospects of a job. I had applied for a job the week you were in New Mexico. One hundred fifty others applied, also. I was the ONLY one they called back and I GOT THE JOB!"

★★★

"I wanted to buy a home for my daughter and me. It would be our first home. I seeded to find the right home. After several fell through, I found it. I got it for one-third off the appraised value by the county. WE LOVE IT!!!"

★★★★

"I had a need and I prayed and asked God to bless me with the finances to do what He had called me to do. My brother called and asked if I needed any money. I said yes!!! He sent it. That was a MIRACLE!"

★★★★

"I heard you on streaming video when you were ministering. I sent an email to the ministry and it was forwarded to you. The next service you prayed for me on streaming video for jobs to come in. My phone started ringing for work…IT WAS A SUNDAY…you don't get those kind of calls on Sunday."

★★★★

"You encouraged me to check my mail even on a Sunday. (God delivers on Sunday. He got in trouble for healing on the Sabbath!) I went to my mailbox and there was a check for $140!!!"

★★★★

"I was believing for money for food for my children. I went to the mailbox and there was a check for $125 from a single man with a note, 'I would rather go without than you or your girls to go without food.' God will supply your every need." This testimony is mine (Joan Hunter).

★★★★

"Someone sent me a thousand dollars for the fourth of July! A blessing for freedom!"

★★★★

Some miscellaneous testimonies:

- Multiple testimonies of $1000 blessings within one month.

- Vehicles were given free of charge within one month.

- Scholarships were awarded.

- Numerous raises and bonuses.

- More houses are selling for those in real estate.

- Self-employed people reporting more clients are coming in every week.

- Back salary was received.

- A house was sold after prayer to loose any hindering forces keeping it from being sold.

★★★★

"I am buying my first house. The price is 33 percent off the appraised value! Thank You, Jesus!"

★★★★

"I am seeding and even my children are getting blessed financially!"

★★★★

"I applied for a job with 50 other applicants. I was the only one called back for a second interview. I got the job!"

★★★★

One day a number of years ago my husband, Kelley's oldest son called us to let us know that he had decided to apply for admission to Harvard University. Kelley had a strong sense from God that his son would be accepted. Kelley said to me, "If he is accepted at Harvard, how will we pay for it?" The per semester cost for attending school at Harvard was more than his yearly earnings before taxes. I told him that if God got him into Harvard He would also have to provide a full ride. In the spring of 2010, his son graduated from Harvard on a full ride!

A Prayer For You

God is just amazing! His blessings are over-whelming and never ending. It is time for you to reach out and receive! Do it now!

I come into alignment with the Word of God concerning you and your family. It is His will for you to prosper. It is God's will for the seed that you sow to INCREASE. It is written in His Word.

"Father, thank You for Your Word. Thank You for freely giving us Your keys to success in this life. Thank You for opening our eyes and hearts to understand Your instruction.

"Father, in response to obedience to Your Word, give the person reading this book exciting, witty inventions and ideas to make money to seed into Your Kingdom. Father, give them wisdom on how to increase what they already have and wisdom on how to spend what You have blessed them with. We will all rejoice and praise You for Your faithfulness in always keeping Your promises. Thank You, Father. In Jesus' name. Amen."

About the Author

Joan Hunter is a compassionate minister, dynamic teacher, accomplished author, and anointed healing evangelist who has devoted her life to carry a message of hope, deliverance, and healing to the nations. As President and Founder of Joan Hunter Ministries and Hearts 4 Him, Joan's vision is to equip believers to take the healing power of God beyond the 4 walls of the church to the 4 corners of the earth.

Having emerged victorious through tragic circumstances, impossible obstacles, and immeasurable devastation, Joan is able to share a message of hope and restoration to the broken hearted, deliverance and freedom to the bound, and healing and wholeness to the diseased. Joan's life is one of uncompromising dedication to the Gospel of Jesus Christ, as she exhibits a sincere desire to see the body of Christ live free, happy, and whole.

Additional Resources

Other books that you can purchase from our on-line store at www.joanhunter.org include:

- *Freedom Through Forgiveness: How True Forgiveness Brings Healing To Every Area Of Your Life*

- *Healing The Heart: Overcoming Betrayal In Your Life*

- *Healing The Whole Man Handbook: Effective Prayers For Body, Soul and Spirit*

- *Healing Starts Now: Comprehensive Manual on Healing*

- *Healings, Miracles and Supernatural Experiences: Healing 4 Haiti*

- *Power To Heal: Experiencing the Miraculous, Healings and Supernatural Phenomena*

- *Preparing For Ministry: Answering God's Call With Confidence*

- *Renewing Relationships: Releasing The Past To Restore Intimacy*

Other resources are available on our Web site or watch Joan's teachings at www.xpmedia.com.